THE

G

M   S

HC   H

HI

THE **TESTING** SERIES
expert advice on test preparation

D0434261

now2become

Orders: Please contact How2become Ltd,
Suite 2, 50 Churchill Square Business Centre, Kings Hill, Kent ME19 4YU.

Telephone: (44) 0845 643 1299 - Lines are open Monday to Friday 9am until 5pm.
Fax: (44) 01732 525965.
You can also order via the email address info@how2become.co.uk.

ISBN 978-1-907558-14-6

First published 2010

Typeset for How2become Ltd by Good Golly Design, Canada, goodgolly.ca.

Printed in Great Britain for How2become Ltd
by Bell & Bain Ltd, 303 Burnfield Road, Thornliebank, Glasgow G46 7UQ.

CONTENTS

WELCOME

Dear Sir/Madam,

Welcome to your new guide, GCSE mathematics: How to pass it with high grades. This guide contains hundreds of GCSE mathematics test questions with highly detailed solutions that are appropriate for anyone revising for their GCSE maths exams and anyone who needs to significantly improve their skills in mathematics.

This guide assumes the reader has very little knowledge of GCSE level mathematics from the very first chapter to the last, which means that you will find it very easy to follow. I have designed this guide so that you are shown how to approach different questions and different scenarios, so that when you are faced with a maths question in the actual exam, you will have a positive attitude and know how to tackle it, using the hints and tips I have provided you with in the guide. The key to success is to try your hardest to get 100% correct answers in the test that you are undertaking. If you aim for 100% in your preparation, then you are far more likely to achieve the grade you desire, which will lead to you gaining more chance of getting your first choice job or university. I have deliberately supplied you with lots of sample questions to assist you. It is crucial that when you get a question wrong, you take the time to find out why you got it wrong. Understanding the question is very important. Follow the examples in each chapter carefully and you will do fine.

Finally, remember that it does not matter what grade you are predicted in mathematics, you are the master of your own destiny. If you want the highest grade that you can personally achieve given the time you have left to revise, read and understand this guide and let change happen.

Good luck and best wishes,

David Isaacs

CHAPTER 1:
INTRODUCTION TO NUMBERS

There are definitions given to different types of numbers. These are useful to know as the exam may refer to the numbers by their definition:

Integers

These are whole numbers i.e. numbers that do not contain any decimals. Integers can be either positive or negative numbers and include zero.

EXAMPLE

-1,-2,-3 are all examples of what are termed as 'negative integers'

1, 2, 3 are all examples of what are termed as 'positive integers'.

Integers are not limited to the above numbers only. Remember that integers define any number which does not have a decimal place.

Prime numbers

These numbers can be divided by the number 1 only to give a whole number (integer) and because of this all prime numbers are greater than 1.

EXAMPLE

Which of the following are prime numbers?

2, 3, 5, 7, 4, 8, 11, 13,

SOLUTION

The trick is to find the numbers which can be divided by 1 only and no other number. These numbers are:

2, 3, 5, 7, 11, 13

The remaining numbers which are divisible by other numbers other than 1 are:

4 and 8

4 can also be divided by 2: $4 \div 2 = 2$

8 can be divided by 4 and 2: $8 \div 4 = 2$ and $8 \div 2 = 4$

Therefore, the number 1 is not the only number 4 and 8 can be divided by meaning that these two numbers are not prime numbers.

Square numbers

These are numbers which can be square rooted. They are produced by multiplying with the same number:

EXAMPLE

5×5=25, I can now say that 25 is a square number, because if I took the square root of 25:

$\sqrt{25}=5$

It equals 5, which was initially multiplied with itself to produce the square number 25.

Surds

These are numbers within a square root that are not square numbers. So for example, $\sqrt{25}$ is not a surd simply because it is a square number whereas the number 10 for example is not a square number and therefore when I put 10 into a square root sign it becomes known as a 'surd'.

EXAMPLE

Which of the following are 'surds':
$\sqrt{6}, \sqrt{5}, \sqrt{36}, \sqrt{4}$

SOLUTION

I know that both 4 and 36 are square numbers:

$2 \times 2 = 4$ *and* $\sqrt{4}=2$

$6 \times 6 = 36$ *and* $\sqrt{36} = 6$

Therefore, the remaining two numbers ($\sqrt{6}$, $\sqrt{5}$) must be surds as they are contained within a square root and are not square numbers

Rational numbers

These are fractions which have a numerator (top half of the fraction) and a denominator (bottom half of the fraction) containing whole (integer) numbers such as 5/8.

Irrational numbers

These are numbers such as π and surds e.g. $\sqrt{5}$ which cannot be written as fractions. If you are not familiar with π, pronounced as 'pie' see the chapter entitled 'circles' later on in this book.

Throughout this book you will come across all the numbers described above and there will be plenty of opportunities to practice using them with the end of chapter practice questions.

CHAPTER 2
MULTIPLICATION

TIMES TABLES

Knowing the times tables forms the basis from which you can improve your mathematical skills in order to do well in exams. Hints and tips are given towards the end of this section to help you memorise the times tables:

The 1 times table:

   1 × 1 = 1

   1 × 2 = 2

   1 × 3 = 3

   1 × 4 = 4

   1 × 5 = 5

   1 × 6 = 6

   1 × 7 = 7

   1 × 8 = 8

   1 × 9 = 9

   1 × 10 = 10

(The 1 times table is the simplest to remember because the answer will always be the number that the 1 is multiplied by)

The 2 times table:

2 × 1 = 2

2 × 2 = 4

2 × 3 = 6

2 × 4 = 8

2 × 5 = 10

2 × 6 = 12

2 × 7 = 14

2 × 8 = 16

2 × 9 = 18

2 × 10 = 20

The 3 times table:

3 × 1 = 3

3 × 2 = 6

3 × 3 = 9

3 × 4 = 12

3 × 5 = 15

3 × 6 = 18

3 × 7 = 21

3 × 8 = 24

3 × 9 = 27

3 × 10 = 30

The 4 times table:

4 × 1 = 4

4 × 2 = 8

4 × 3 = 12

4 × 4 = 16

4 × 5 = 20

4 × 6 = 24

4 × 7 = 28

4 × 8 = 32

4 × 9 = 36

4 × 10 = 40

The 5 times table:

5 × 1 = 5

5 × 2 = 10

5 × 3 = 15

5 × 4 = 20

5 × 5 = 25

5 × 6 = 30

5 × 7 = 35

5 × 8 = 40

5 × 9 = 45

5 × 10 = 50

The 6 times table:

6 × 1 = 6

6 × 2 = 12

6 × 3 = 18

6 × 4 = 24

6 × 5 = 30

6 × 6 = 36

6 × 7 = 42

6 × 8 = 48

6 × 9 = 54

6 × 10 = 60

The 7 times table:

7 × 1 = 7

7 × 2 = 14

7 × 3 = 21

7 × 4 = 28

7 × 5 = 35

7 × 6 = 42

7 × 7 = 49

7 × 8 = 56

7 × 9 = 63

7 × 10 = 70

The 8 times table:

8 × 1 = 8

8 × 2 = 16

8 × 3 = 24

8 × 4 = 32

8 × 5 = 40

8 × 6 = 48

8 × 7 = 56

8 × 8 = 64

8 × 9 = 72

8 × 10 = 80

The 9 times table:

9 × 1 = 9

9 × 2 = 18

9 × 3 = 27

9 × 4 = 36

9 × 5 = 45

9 × 6 = 54

9 × 7 = 63

9 × 8 = 72

9 × 9 = 81

9 × 10 = 90

The 10 times table:

10 × 1 = 10

10 × 2 = 20

10 × 3 = 30

10 × 4 = 40

10 × 5 = 50

10 × 6 = 60

10 × 7 = 70

10 × 8 = 80

10 × 9 = 90

10 × 10 = 100

(The answer for all numbers multiplied by 10 is to have one zero added to the end of the number being multiplied by 10)

SUMMARY TABLE FOR REFERENCE:

	1	2	3	4	5	6	7	8	9	10
1	1	2	3	4	5	6	7	8	9	10
2	2	4	6	8	10	12	14	16	18	20
3	3	6	9	12	15	18	21	24	27	30
4	4	8	12	16	20	24	28	32	36	40
5	5	10	15	20	25	30	35	40	45	50
6	6	12	18	24	30	36	42	48	54	60
7	7	14	21	28	35	42	49	56	63	70
8	8	16	24	32	40	48	56	64	72	80
9	9	18	27	36	45	54	63	72	81	90
10	10	20	30	40	50	60	70	80	90	100

The numbers in black shows the result of the numbers in gray i.e. the vertical column multiplied by the horizontal row.

HINTS AND TIPS FOR MEMORISING THE TIMES TABLES:

'Practice makes perfect'. Nothing is more true when it comes to multiplication!. Personally, I found that after going through questions involving multiplication I began to memorise the answers to certain numbers which are multiplied together. Eventually, after continual practice with multiplication questions, I found that I had learnt my times tables. There is absolutely no reason why the same cannot happen to you when you practice questions involving multiplication. The end of chapter questions below will help you towards memorising your times tables.

The following explains how I first began learning the times tables:

I knew for any times table a multiplication by 1 would not change the number being multiplied by 1 e.g. $1 \times 2 = 2$

I also knew that the times table for a particular number increases by that number each time e.g. The 2 times table increases by 2:

$$\left.\begin{array}{l} 2 \times 1 = 2 \\ 2 \times 2 = 4 \end{array}\right\} +2$$

This meant that I could now work out any multiplication question given to me. For example, if I was asked to calculate 2×4 I would have begun at 2 × 1 = 2 and added 2 to the answer of 2 × 1, which is 2, another three times to get to the answer of 2 × 4 = 8. Try it for yourself and see that it works.

Equally, you may find that you have memorised a multiplication that does not belong to the 1 times table such as 6 × 8 = 48 for example.

This is useful to you because it means that you can now calculate the answers to multiplications either lower or higher than the one you have memorised. For example, if you had memorised 6 × 8 = 48 and needed to find the answer to 6×7 you would have to subtract 6 from 48:

$$\left.\begin{array}{l} 6 \times 8 = 48 \\ 6 \times 7 = 42 \end{array}\right\} \text{-6}$$

This method can be used for all times tables, providing you memorise the answer to at least one multiplication sum from each times table. Please note that this advice is only to get you started learning your times tables.

Once you start using the times tables over and over again when practicing mathematical problems, you will memorise them and not need to have to go through the above methods each and every time.

However, it is better to learn the times tables as soon as you can so that you do not waste valuable time in your exam having to add or subtract numbers to get the multiplication answer you need.

Remember, I am a human just like you. If I did it, you can do it. It is vital that you learn the times tables up to and including the 9 times table because once you have learnt them, you will be able to solve any other multiplications using long multiplication (see 'long multiplication' below).

Now have a go at filling in the empty boxes (answers at the back of the book).

TIMES TABLES QUESTIONS:

1. $2 \times 2 =$ __   Answer ☐

2. $2 \times$ __ $= 18$ Answer ☐

3. $10 \times 4 =$ __0 Answer ☐

4. $9 \times 9 = 8$ __   Answer ☐

5. $10 \times 10 = 10$ __   Answer ☐

6. $3 \times$ __ $= 6$ Answer ☐

7. __ $\times 7 = 63$ Answer ☐

8. $8 \times$ __ $= 56$ Answer ☐

9. $7 \times 8 = 5$__   Answer ☐

10. $3 \times 3 =$ __   Answer ☐

11. $6 \times 7 = 4$__   Answer ☐

12. $7 \times$__ $= 49$ Answer ☐

13. $6 \times 5 = 3$__   Answer ☐

14. $5 \times 5 =$ __5 Answer ☐

15. $3 \times 4 = 1$__   Answer ☐

16. $4 \times$ __ $= 20$ Answer ☐

17. $5 \times$ __ $= 20$ Answer ☐

18. $4 \times$ __ $= 28$ Answer ☐

19. $2 \times 4 =$ __   Answer ☐

20. $3 \times 10 =$ __0 Answer ☐

21. $2 \times$ __ $= 2$ Answer ☐

22. $3 \times 1 =$ __   Answer ☐

23. $1 \times 4 =$ __   Answer ☐

24. __ $\times 1 = 5$ Answer ☐

25. $9 \times$ __ $= 45$ Answer ☐

26. $9 \times 6 = 5$__   Answer ☐

CHAPTER 3
LONG MULTIPLICATION

Long multiplication becomes useful in the following scenarios:

- When one number being multiplied has one digit and the other number that it is multiplied with has two or more digits e.g. 2 × 10 or 2 × 100 etc.

- When both numbers being multiplied contain two or more digits e.g. 13 × 12 or 132 × 12 or any other combination of numbers containing two or more digits etc.

For the following examples, the numbers which are being multiplied are shown circled for explanation purposes.

EXAMPLE
Calculate the following, showing all working out:

a) 32 × 5

b) 16 × 3

c) 10 × 2

SOLUTION
a) Your first thoughts about this question might be that the previous section on multiplication only went up to the 10 times table and not the 32 times

table. The good news is that it doesn't matter!. In fact, you only need to know your times tables up to the 10 times table to work out such a multiplication and I will show you how to do this below:

In order to show my working out, I must first present the question in a way that I can use to help me work out the question. This means putting the highest number being multiplied above the lowest, with the number below pushed to the right hand side as shown:

$$
\begin{array}{r}
3\,2 \\
\times\,5 \\
\hline
\end{array}
$$

The numbers are now ready to be multiplied when in this format. I begin the multiplication using the two numbers furthest to the right hand side i.e. the 2 and the 5:

$$2 \times 5 = 10$$

Underneath the line, I must now put the result which is 10. However, I only put one digit of the number 10 under the line, which is the zero of 10 (the right hand digit) and the 1 from the left hand side of the number 10 is forwarded as a remainder (indicated by the small 1 next to the 3 on the left hand side) which will be added to the next multiplication to be done. So far, the multiplication looks like:

$$
\begin{array}{r}
3^{1}2 \\
\times\,5 \\
\hline
0
\end{array}
$$

The next step is to multiply the top left number with the number on the lower part of the multiplication i.e. multiply the 3 and 5:

$$3 \times 5 = 15$$

At this point I add the remainder of 1 to the 15:

$$15 + 1 = 16$$

Because there are no further multiplications to be done I can now put the whole answer of 16 under the line and not just the right hand side digit as I did for the 10. The multiplication now looks like:

$$
\begin{array}{r}
3\,2 \\
\times\,5 \\
\hline
1\,6\,0
\end{array}
$$

The final answer is 160 and I have shown all working out although in an exam you will not need to write things like 2 × 5 = 10 or 15 + 1 = 16, simply because by writing the answer below the line you have shown that you are able to calculate the multiplication question. However if it helps you to work out the question, writing out every step will not lose you any marks so feel free to do this if you wish.

b) 16 × 3 =

As done in a) above, the multiplication must be written in the form:

$$\begin{array}{r} 1\,6 \\ \times\,3 \\ \hline \end{array}$$

I will now begin the multiplication by multiplying the top right number with the number on the bottom i.e. the 6 and the 3 circled below:

$$6 \times 3 = 18$$

As before, 18 cannot go under the line as there is one more multiplication to be done and only the number 8 from the right digit of the number 18 can be put under the line. The 1 from the left hand side of the number 18 is given as a remainder (shown in small next to the top left number 1 in the multiplication below):

$$\begin{array}{r} 1^{1}6 \\ \times\,3 \\ \hline 8 \end{array}$$

I now multiply the next and final two numbers which are 1 and 3 shown in circled below:

$$\begin{array}{r} ①\!6 \\ \times\,③ \\ \hline 8 \end{array}$$

$$1 \times 3 = 3$$

Remember that there is also a remainder of 1 to be added onto the 3 which came from the 1 in the number 18:

$$3 + 1 = 4$$

The 4 can be put straight under the line along with 8 because there are no further multiplications to be carried out:

$$\begin{array}{r} 1\ 6 \\ \times\ 3 \\ \hline 4\ 8 \end{array}$$

The final answer is 48. Isn't it amazing that you only need to memorise the times tables up to 10 in order to be able to calculate any multiplication!.

c) 10 × 2 =

Although you may know how to solve this without doing a long multiplication, I will work this question out using long multiplication anyway so that you can see the simplicity of using long multiplication.

The first step to take is to prepare for a long multiplication by putting the numbers one above the other:

I must now multiply the top right digit with the digit below it i.e. 0 and 2 (shown above in circles):

$$0 \times 2 = 0$$

This question is easier than questions a) and b) above as there is now no remainder to deal with and so the 0 goes straight under the line:

$$\begin{array}{r} 1\ 0 \\ \times\ 2 \\ \hline 0 \end{array}$$

The final multiplication is the 1 from the number 10 and the 2 below it (circled below):

$$\begin{array}{r} ①0 \\ \times② \\ \hline 0 \end{array}$$

$$1 \times 2 = 2$$

The 2 goes straight under the line to join the 0:

$$\begin{array}{r} 1\ 0 \\ \times\ 2 \\ \hline 2\ 0 \end{array}$$

The final answer is therefore 20. You would not normally need to do long multiplication to calculate 10 × 2. The answer can be found by adding a zero to the end of the 2. This applies to any number multiplied by 10: simply add a zero to the end of the number being multiplied by 10.

The next few examples aim to introduce you to solving numbers multiplied with 2 digits or more on both the top and bottom rows and will also show you how to deal with decimals when multiplying.

EXAMPLE

Calculate the following, showing all working out:

  a) 32 × 33

  b) 3.2 × 3.3

  c) 567 × 23

  d) 5.67 × 2.3

  e) 132 × 245

  f) 13.2 × 2.45

SOLUTIONS

a) 32 × 33

For a question which has two numbers multiplied together containing the same number of digits (2 in this case), there will be no need to select which number goes on the top row in order to carry out a long multiplication.
I could write the question out as:

$$\begin{array}{r} 3\,2 \\ \times\ 3\,3 \\ \hline \end{array} \quad \text{or} \quad \begin{array}{r} 3\,3 \\ \times\ 3\,2 \\ \hline \end{array}$$

Using any of the two above will produce the same answer. I will use the first to carry out the multiplication for no reason other than I had to choose one of the two.

The first thing I must do is to multiply the top right digit (2) with the bottom right digit (3), circled below:

$$\begin{array}{r} 3\,②\\ \times\ 3\,③\\ \hline \end{array}$$

$$2 \times 3 = 6$$

The 6 is one digit and can therefore be put straight under the line. Being only one digit I know that there are no remainders to carry forward:

$$\begin{array}{r} 3\,2\\ \times\ 3\,3\\ \hline 6 \end{array}$$

The next step I must take is to multiply the number 3 on the top left with the number 3 on the bottom right (circled below):

$$\begin{array}{r} ③\,2\\ \times\ 3\,③\\ \hline 6 \end{array}$$

$$3 \times 3 = 9$$

This result can be put straight under the line again to join the 6:

$$\begin{array}{r} 3\,2\\ \times\ 3\,3\\ \hline 9\,6 \end{array}$$

The next step is to multiply the two digits on the top (3 and 2) with the bottom left digit (3) separately. It is important when doing long multiplication to work from right to left, so I will have to start by multiplying the 2 on the top right with the 3 on the bottom left (circled below):

$$\begin{array}{r} 3\,②\\ \times\ ③\,3\\ \hline 9\,6 \end{array}$$

$$2 \times 3 = 6$$

This 6 now goes under the 9 already in place:

$$\begin{array}{r} 3\,2\\ \times\ 3\,3\\ \hline 9\,6\\ 6 \end{array}$$

Notice the 6 has been pushed to the left by 1 figure and now goes under the 9. This is standard procedure when multiplying two numbers which both have two digits or more.

The final multiplication to be carried out is the top left 3 with the bottom left 3 (circled below):

$$
\begin{array}{r}
\textcircled{3}2 \\
\times\ \textcircled{3}3 \\
\hline
9\,6 \\
6
\end{array}
$$

$$3 \times 3 = 9$$

This 9 goes to the left of the 6. The plus sign below is shown to indicate that anything below the first line needs to be added to give the final answer:

$$
\begin{array}{r}
3\,2 \\
\times\ 3\,3 \\
\hline
+\,9\,6 \\
9\,6 \\
\hline
\end{array}
$$

I can now treat the numbers below the first line as a long addition question which needs to be calculated. Isolating just the numbers below the first line from above I have:

$$
\begin{array}{r}
9\,6 \\
+\,9\,6 \\
\hline
\end{array}
$$

Starting from the right hand side, I have a 6 to deal with which is located in the top right. There is nothing to add to the 6. I know this because there is nothing below the 6 which is located on the top row. So far I have:

$$
\begin{array}{r}
9\,6 \\
+\,9\,6 \\
\hline
6
\end{array}
$$

Moving left from the top right hand 6, I have a 9 to deal with which needs to be added to the 6 beneath it:

$$9 + 6 = 15$$

Because the number 15 is two digits long, only the right hand digit can be put underneath the line and the left hand digit becomes a remainder. Therefore, the number 5 is put under the line and the 1 becomes a remainder (indicated by a small 1 located next to the 9 on the bottom left):

$$
\begin{array}{r}
9\,6 \\
+\ 9\,^{1}6 \\
\hline
5\,6
\end{array}
$$

Moving to the left for the last time, there is nothing on the top row and a 9 on the bottom row with a remainder of 1 next to it. I must now add 1(the remainder) to 9:

$$1 + 9 = 10$$

Because there are no further digits to add, the number 10 can go straight under the line giving a final answer of:

$$
\begin{array}{r}
9\,6 \\
+\ 9\,^{1}6 \\
\hline
1\,0\,5\,6
\end{array}
$$

Going back to the multiplication, the entire working out looks like:

$$
\begin{array}{r}
3\,2 \\
\times\ 3\,3 \\
\hline
9\,6 \\
+\ 9\,^{1}6 \\
\hline
1\,0\,5\,6
\end{array}
$$

The answer to 32 × 33 is **1056**

In summary, the numbers I have multiplied are shown in order below. The trend is to multiply the digit on the right in the bottom row by all digits in the top row. Once this is done, the next digit to the left on the bottom row, 3 in this case, is multiplied by all digits in the top row:

b) 3.2 × 3.3

To answer this question, I firstly ignore the fact that there are decimal places in the question and calculate the question as if there were no decimal places in the first place i.e. I calculate 32 × 33. I have calculated this already in the previous example and the answer is 1056.

Now that I know the answer to 32 × 33 is 1056, I can add decimal places as required. To find where to put in decimal places, I examine the two numbers that are being multiplied for this question:

3.2 × 3.3

I need to look at both numbers individually. So, starting with 3.2, I can see that the decimal point is located one digit from the right hand side:

3.2

The decimal place is located one digit away from the right hand side of 3.2

Looking at 3.3, it is the same situation (the decimal place is located 1 digit away from the right). In total, with both decimals being 1 digit away from the right of both 3.2 and 3.3, I have 1 + 1 = 2 decimal places.

I can now look at the answer to 32 × 33 again, which is 1056 and starting from the right hand side of 1056, go in two decimal places to the left (two decimal places because both the numbers being multiplied in this example were a total of two away from the right hand side). This will bring the decimal place to rest between the 0 and the 5. The final answer is:

3.2×3.3=10.56

c) 567 × 23

To carry out this multiplication, I must put the number with the most digits on the top row, 567 in this case and the number containing the least digits (23) below it, making sure that both the top and bottom numbers are aligned to the right:

$$
\begin{array}{r}
5\,6\,7 \\
\times\,2\,3 \\
\hline
\end{array}
$$

I can now begin the multiplication by firstly multiplying the 3 on the bottom right with all the numbers on the top row separately. I begin with the top right number, which is 7. Multiplying this with the bottom right number, 3 gives:

$$5\ 6\ ⑦$$
$$\times\ 2\ ③$$

$$7 \times 3 = 21$$

Remember that only one digit can go under the line as there are more multiplications to be carried out. Therefore, the 1 from the number 21 goes under the line and the number 2 from the number 21 is put forward as a remainder (indicated below, next to the 6):

$$5\ 6^2 7$$
$$\times\ 2\ 3$$
$$\overline{\qquad 1}$$

Moving left, I now multiply the 6 on the top row with the 3 on the bottom left:

$$5\ ⑥^2 7$$
$$\times\ 2\ ③$$
$$\overline{\qquad 1}$$

$$6 \times 3 = 18$$

I can also see that there is a remainder of 2 beside the 6, which means I need to add 2 to this answer:

$$18 + 2 = 20$$

As before, only one digit from the number 20 can go under the line and that digit will always be the one furthest to the right. In this case, the digit furthest to the right on the number 20 is 0 which means 0 goes under the line while the 2 from the left hand side of the number 20 gets put forward as a remainder (indicated by a small 2 beside the number 5):

$$5^2 6\ 7$$
$$\times\ 2\ 3$$
$$\overline{\qquad 0\ 1}$$

The only remaining number from the top row to be multiplied with the 3 on the right hand side of the bottom row is the number 5

$$
\begin{array}{r}
⑤^2 6\ 7 \\
\times\ 2③ \\
\hline
0\ 1
\end{array}
$$

$$5 \times 3 = 15$$

I also know that there is a remainder of 2 to be added onto this, which gives:

$$15 + 2 = 17$$

I still need to multiply the entire top row of numbers with the 2 on the bottom left one by one. However, when I do this, the answers will form a second row under the numbers already beneath the line and so the answer of 17 I just calculated is the last answer for the first row beneath the line and I can therefore put the whole of the number 17 beneath the line as shown below:

$$
\begin{array}{r}
5\ 6\ 7 \\
\times\ 2\ 3 \\
\hline
1\ 7\ 0\ 1
\end{array}
$$

This is not the final answer. I will now multiply all the top row numbers with the 2 on the bottom row separately.

Working from right to left, I start with the 7 on the top row:

$$
\begin{array}{r}
5\ 6⑦ \\
\times②3 \\
\hline
1\ 7\ 0\ 1
\end{array}
$$

$$7 \times 2 = 14$$

When starting a second row, always go in one digit from the right. This means that the number 4 from 14 will go beneath the 0 in 1701 and the number 1 from the left hand side of the number 14 is put forward as a remainder (indicated by a small 1 next to the number 6 on the top row):

$$5\ 6^17$$
$$\times\ 2\ 3$$
$$\overline{1\ 7\ 0\ 1}$$
$$4$$

Moving to the left, the next number on the top row, 6, must be multiplied with the 2 on the bottom row:

$$5⑥^17$$
$$\times②3$$
$$\overline{1\ 7\ 0\ 1}$$
$$4$$

$$6 \times 2 = 12$$

I must now add the remainder of 1:

$$12 + 1 = 13$$

Because there is still one more multiplication to carry out, only the number 3 from the number 13 can be put on the second row under the number 7 and the number 1 from the left hand side of the number 13 becomes a remainder:

$$5^16\ 7$$
$$\times\ 2\ 3$$
$$\overline{1\ 7\ 0\ 1}$$
$$3\ 4$$

The next and final step is to multiply the 5 in the top left corner by the 2 on the bottom left:

$$⑤^16\ 7$$
$$\times②3$$
$$\overline{1\ 7\ 0\ 1}$$
$$3\ 4$$

$$5 \times 2 = 10$$

I also know there is a remainder of 1 to be added to this:

$$10 + 1 = 11$$

Because this is the final multiplication to be carried out, the whole of the number 11 can go on the second row under the line:

$$
\begin{array}{r}
5\ 6\ 7 \\
\times\ 2\ 3 \\
\hline
1\ 7\ 0\ 1 \\
1\ 1\ 3\ 4 \\
\hline
\end{array}
$$

The next step is to add everything below the first line, which is:

$$
\begin{array}{r}
+\ 1\ 7\ 0\ 1 \\
1\ 1\ 3\ 4 \\
\hline
\end{array}
$$

Starting from the right, the 1 can be brought below the line directly.

$$
\begin{array}{r}
+\ 1\ 7\ 0\ 1 \\
1\ 1\ 3\ 4 \downarrow \\
\hline
1 \\
\end{array}
$$

Moving left, 0 is added to 4 (circled below):

$$
\begin{array}{r}
+\ 1\ 7\ ⓪\ 1 \\
1\ 1\ 3\ ④ \\
\hline
1 \\
\end{array}
$$

$$0+4=4$$

Moving left again, 7 is added to 3:

$$
\begin{array}{r}
+\ 1\ ⑦\ 0\ 1 \\
1\ 1\ ③\ 4 \\
\hline
1 \\
\end{array}
$$

$$7 + 3 = 10$$

As this is not the final addition, only the zero from 10 can go beneath the line with the 1 being put forward as a remainder. So far we have:

```
    5 6 7
  × 2 3
  1¹7 0 1
1 1 3 4
    0 4 1
```

The next numbers to add are the two 1s: 1 + 1 = 2

```
    5 6 7
  × 2 3
  ⑴7 0 1
1⑴3 4
    0 4 1
```

Also remember to add the remainder of 1:

$$2 + 1 = 3$$

Therefore, 3 now goes beneath the line:

```
    5 6 7
  × 2 3
  1¹7 0 1
1 1 3 4
  3 0 4 1
```

Moving left again, there is a number 1 on its own. This can simply be brought beneath the line:

```
    5 6 7
  × 2 3
  1 7 0 1
1 1 3 4
1 3 0 4 1
```

The final answer to the multiplication is 13041.

d) 5.67 × 2.3

Remember that with multiplications containing decimal places, it is best to calculate the multiplication as if there were no decimal places involved as done above and once this is done it is easier to add any decimal places.

For this question, I can see that the decimal on **5.67** is located 2 digits in from the right and the decimal on **2.3** is located one digit in from the right. Therefore, the total amount of digits from the right that the decimal point will be placed on 13041 is 2 + 1 = 3.

The answer to 567 × 23 is 13041. Placing a decimal point 3 digits in from the right would mean that there will be a decimal point between the 3 and the 0:

$$1\,3\,.\,0\,4\,1$$

The answer to the question is **5.67 × 2.3 = 13.041**

e) 132×245

As both numbers contain an equal number of digits, it does not matter which number I put on the top row first. I start by writing out the multiplication in a format I can work with:

$$
\begin{array}{r}
1\,3\,2 \\
\times\,2\,4\,5 \\
\hline
\end{array}
$$

I must now multiply all digits in the top row with the number 5 located on the right hand side of the bottom row separately. Working from right to left, I start with the 2 on the top right hand side and multiply this by the 5 on the bottom right:

$$
\begin{array}{r}
1\,3\,②\\
\times\,2\,4\,⑤\\
\hline
\end{array}
$$

$$5 \times 2 = 10$$

Only the zero from the 10 goes beneath the line and the 1 gets put forward as a remainder:

$$
\begin{array}{r}
1\,3^{1}2 \\
\times\,2\,4\,5 \\
\hline
0
\end{array}
$$

Moving left, the next digit to be multiplied with the number 5 is the 3:

$$1\,\textcircled{3}\overset{1}{2}$$
$$\times\,2\,4\,\textcircled{5}$$
$$\overline{\hphantom{xxxx}0}$$

$$5 \times 3 = 15$$

There is also a remainder of 1 to be added onto this:

$$15 + 1 = 16$$

As this is not the final multiplication that will take place involving the number 5, I can only put the number 6 from the right of the number 16 under the line and the 1 from the left hand side of the number 16 becomes a remainder:

$$1\overset{1}{\,}3\,2$$
$$\times\,2\,4\,5$$
$$\overline{\hphantom{xx}6\,0}$$

Moving left again, I now multiply the 1 from the top row with the 5 on the bottom row:

$$\textcircled{1}\overset{1}{3}\,2$$
$$\times\,2\,4\,\textcircled{5}$$
$$\overline{\hphantom{xx}6\,0}$$

$$1 \times 5 = 5$$

There is also a remainder of 1 to be added onto this: $5 + 1 = 6$

This number goes straight under the line:

$$1\,3\,2$$
$$\times\,2\,4\,5$$
$$\overline{6\,6\,0}$$

Next, I must multiply the 4 on the bottom row by all digits on the top row. Working from right to left again on the top row I will first multiply the 2 from the top row with the 4 on the bottom row:

```
    1 3 ②
  × 2 ④ 5
  ─────────
    6 6 0
```

$$2 \times 4 = 8$$

Remember that every time a new digit from the bottom row is multiplied with a number from the top row, the answer is placed one character in from the right below the first row of answers:

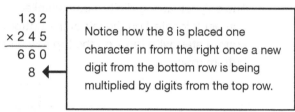

```
    1 3 2
  × 2 4 5
  ─────────
    6 6 0
        8
```

Notice how the 8 is placed one character in from the right once a new digit from the bottom row is being multiplied by digits from the top row.

Moving to the next digit on the top row, I now multiply 3 with the 4 on the bottom row:

```
    1 ③ 2
  × 2 ④ 5
  ─────────
    6 6 0
        8
```

$$4 \times 3 = 12$$

Because there remains one more digit to be multiplied with the 4 on the bottom row, only the 2 from the 12 can be put below the line and the 1 from the 12 becomes a remainder:

```
    1 3 2
  × 2 4 5
  ─────────
    6 6 0
      2 8
```

Finally, I multiply the 1 on the left of the top row with the 4 on the bottom row:

```
    ① 3 2
  × 2 ④ 5
  ─────────
    6 6 0
      2 8
```

$$1 \times 4 = 4$$

There is also a remainder of 1 to be added: $4 + 1 = 5$

This can now go straight under the line to join the 2 and 8:

$$
\begin{array}{r}
1\ 3\ 2 \\
\times\ 2\ 4\ 5 \\
\hline
6\ 6\ 0 \\
5\ 2\ 8
\end{array}
$$

The only remaining digit to be multiplied by the digits on the top row is the number 2 located on the left of the bottom row. Working from right to left again, I start with the 2 on the top row and multiply this by the 2 on the bottom row:

$$
\begin{array}{r}
1\ 3\ ②\ \\
×②4\ 5 \\
\hline
6\ 6\ 0 \\
5\ 2\ 8
\end{array}
$$

$$2 \times 2 = 4$$

Because a new digit is being multiplied from the bottom row, the number 4 will be placed one character in from the right again:

$$
\begin{array}{r}
1\ 3\ 2 \\
\times\ 2\ 4\ 5 \\
\hline
6\ 6\ 0 \\
5\ 2\ 8 \\
4\quad
\end{array}
$$

Notice how the 4 is placed one character in from the right once a new digit from the bottom row is being multiplied by digits from the top row.

Moving to the left, I now multiply the 3 from the top row with the 2 on the bottom row:

$$
\begin{array}{r}
1③2 \\
×②4\ 5 \\
\hline
6\ 6\ 0 \\
5\ 2\ 8 \\
6\ 4\quad
\end{array}
$$

$3 \times 2 = 6$, leading to a 6 being placed to the left of the 4:

```
    1 3 2
  × 2 4 5
    6 6 0
  5 2 8
  6 4
  _____
```

Finally I multiply the 1 on the top row with the 2 on the bottom row:

```
   ①3 2
  ×②4 5
    6 6 0
  5 2 8
  6 4
  _____
```

1×2=2

This gives:

```
    1 3 2
  × 2 4 5
    6 6 0
  5 2 8
  2 6 4
  _____
```

To find the final answer, I need to add all the numbers below the first line:

Working from right to left, the first column contains a zero. This can go straight under the second line:

```
    1 3 2
  × 2 4 5
    6 6 0
  5 2 8
  2 6 4
  _____
        0
```

Moving left, the next column contains an 8 and a 6:

8 + 6 = 14

Only the 4 from the number 14 can go under the line, with the 1 from the number 14 becoming a remainder:

$$
\begin{array}{r}
1\ 3\ 2 \\
\times\ 2\ 4\ 5 \\
\hline
6\,{}^{1}6\ 0 \\
5\ 2\ 8 \\
2\ 6\ 4 \\
\hline
4\ 0
\end{array}
$$

Moving on, the next column to the left contains a 6 with a remainder of 1 (in brackets below), a 2 and a 4, giving a total of:

$$6 + (1) + 2 + 4 = 13$$

Only the 3 from the 13 can go beneath the line, with the 1 from the number 13 being used as a remainder in the next column to the left:

$$
\begin{array}{r}
1\ 3\ 2 \\
\times\ 2\ 4\ 5 \\
\hline
6\ 6\ 0 \\
5\,{}^{1}2\ 8 \\
2\ 6\ 4 \\
\hline
3\ 4\ 0
\end{array}
$$

Moving to the next column, I have a 5 with a remainder of 1 (shown below in brackets) and a 6, giving a total of:

$$5 + (1) + 6 = 12$$

Once again, because this is not the final addition to be made, only the 2 can go beneath the line from the number 12 with the 1 being carried forward to the next column on the left as a remainder:

$$
\begin{array}{r}
1\ 3\ 2 \\
\times\ 2\ 4\ 5 \\
\hline
6\ 6\ 0 \\
5\ 2\ 8 \\
2\,{}^{1}6\ 4 \\
\hline
2\ 3\ 4\ 0
\end{array}
$$

Moving to the next and final column on the left, I have a 2 with a remainder of 1 (shown in brackets below), giving a total of:

$$2 + (1) = 3$$

This goes straight under the line as it is the final addition, giving a final answer of:

$$
\begin{array}{r}
1\,3\,2 \\
\times\,2\,4\,5 \\
\hline
6\,6\,0 \\
5\,2\,8 \\
2\,6\,4 \\
\hline
3\,2\,3\,4\,0
\end{array}
$$

Therefore the final answer to this multiplication question is **32340**.

f) 13.2 × 2.45

To solve this question I once again count how many digits from the right the decimal place is located on both the numbers being multiplied (13.2 and 2.45).

For 13.2, the decimal point is located one digit in from the right and for 2.45, the decimal point is located 2 digits in from the right making a total of 1 + 2 = 3 decimal places.

Therefore, 3 is the amount of digits that I need to place the decimal point in from the right of 32340, which is the answer to 132 × 245. This will bring the decimal place between the 2 and 3 in 32340, which leads to the answer to g):

$$13.2 \times 2.45 = 32.340$$

Isn't it a great feeling knowing that you can now get the answer to any multiplication question you are faced with!

CONCLUDING REMARKS

It does not matter how long the numbers that need to be multiplied are. As long as you stick to the methods shown above, you will be able to calculate any multiplication.

Remember to work from right to left. It is important to start with the number most to the right on the bottom row and multiply this by all the digits contained in the top row separately. Repeat this process until all digits in the bottom row have been multiplied with the top row digits. Remember to indent the number by one digit from the right every time a new digit on the bottom row is multiplied with the top digits.

When a multiplication question appears to have decimal points, the action to take is to ignore the decimal points and carry out the multiplication as if there were no decimal points to begin with. Once you establish an answer to the question as if it never had decimal points, you can return to the original question which did have decimal points. The trick is to count how many digits from the right the decimal point is for each number being multiplied separately and total them. This total tells you the amount you need to move inwards from the right of the answer you calculated while imagining there to be no decimal places.

END OF CHAPTER QUESTIONS (LONG MULTIPLICATION)

Do not use a calculator for the following questions. If you get stuck, return to the examples in this chapter and find an example that is similar to the question you are stuck with for guidance. There is no better way to build your confidence then to work out the questions unaided.

1. 11×11

2. 13×12

3. 25×35

4. 13×2

5. 15×9

6. 18×5

7. 16×6

8. 225×3

9. 145×5

10. 712×4

11. 71.2×4

12. 7.12×4

13. 0.712 × 4

14. 0.712 × 0.4

15. 132 × 246

16. 210 × 51

17. 1.56 × 2.44

18. 148 × 5

19. 23 × 2

20. 0.23 × 2

21. 0.23 × 0.2

CHAPTER 4
LONG DIVISION

Long division becomes easy once you are familiar with the times tables. Let's go through some examples. Remember that a division does not mean that the answer will always be a whole number. It could turn out to have decimal places also and this occurs as a result of remainders. This chapter aims to get you familiar with long division in all its forms.

EXAMPLE
Calculate 10÷2 showing all working out

SOLUTION
Firstly, I must write this in the correct format for a long division which is:

$$2\sqrt{10}$$

The symbol $\sqrt{\dots}$ is called a division sign i.e. the symbol the number 10 is enclosed by. To calculate this, I know that 5 × 2 = 10 which means 2 goes into 10 five times.

I can therefore put a 5 above the division sign as shown below to indicate that the number 2 goes into 10 five times:

$$\frac{5}{2\sqrt{10}}$$

The next step in any division question is to multiply the number on top of the division sign by the number outside of it. For this particular question, I must now multiply the 5 on top of the division sign with the 2 outside of it (circled below for clarity):

$$\frac{\circled{5}}{\circled{2}\sqrt{10}}$$

Once I have calculated the multiplication of the numbers circled above, which is $5 \times 2 = 10$, the result of the multiplication goes beneath the numbers located within the division sign ready to be subtracted:

$$
\begin{array}{r}
5 \\
2\sqrt{10} \\
5 \times 2 = \circled{10}
\end{array}
\left.\begin{array}{c} \\ \\ \end{array}\right\}
$$

These two numbers are now ready to be subtracted.

Note that I have only included the multiplication which appears as (5×2) with its answer of 10 circled above as an aid for explanation. In an exam, I would have written the long division up to this point as:

$$
\begin{array}{r}
5 \\
2\sqrt{10} \\
\underline{10}
\end{array}
$$

The next step is to subtract:

$$10 - 10 = 0$$

The answer of zero indicates that there are no remainders and that the long division stops here:

$$
\begin{array}{r}
5 \\
2\sqrt{10} \\
\underline{10} \\
0
\end{array}
$$

The answer to this example is 5 and all working out has been shown. The following example shows the technique for dealing with remainders i.e. when the subtraction does not conveniently turn out to be zero as it did for this example.

EXAMPLE
Calculate $135 \div 2$

SOLUTION
Firstly I must write this question in a form that I am able to work with:

$$2\sqrt{135}$$

I know that 2 cannot go into 1, so I put a zero above the 1 inside the division sign:

$$\frac{0}{2\sqrt{135}}$$

As must be done for all long divisions, the number on top of a division sign needs to be multiplied with the number outside of it. In this case, I need to multiply the 0 on top of the division sign with the 2 outside of it (circled below):

$$\frac{\textcircled{0}}{\textcircled{2}\sqrt{135}}$$

$$2 \times 0 = 0$$

The zero is now put under the 1 ready to be subtracted:

$$\frac{0}{2\sqrt{135}}$$
$$\underline{0}$$

$$1 - 0 = 1$$

The division now looks like:

$$\frac{0}{2\sqrt{135}}$$
$$\underline{0}$$
$$1$$

The 1 is known as a remainder. When doing long division and the number outside the division sign cannot go into a certain number, it is standard practice to 'borrow' the next number. The next digit is the number 3 from 135. To borrow it, I will need to bring it down to join the 1 currently on its own to make the number 13:

$$\frac{5}{2\sqrt{135}}$$
$$0\downarrow$$
$$13$$

I can now ask myself how many times 2 goes into 13. A quick tip for answering this is to know which number will multiply with 2 giving an answer closest to 13 but at the same time not exceed 13. The answer is 6 in this case, 6 × 2 = 12.

I can now put a 6 directly above the 3:

$$\begin{array}{r} 06 \\ 2\overline{)135} \end{array}$$

Multiplying the 6 with the 2 gives 12 which will go under the 13 ready to be subtracted:

$$\begin{array}{r} 0\,⑥ \\ ②\overline{)135} \\ 0 \\ \overline{13} \\ 12 \\ \overline{1} \end{array}$$

Subtracting the 13 and 12, the answer is 1 again, which means I have to 'borrow' the next number, which is a 5. I 'borrow' the 5 (in bold below) by bringing it down to join the 1 on its own:

$$\begin{array}{r} 06 \\ 2\overline{)1\mathbf{35}} \\ 0 \\ \overline{13} \\ 12 \\ \overline{\mathbf{15}} \end{array}$$

I can now ask myself how many times 2 goes into 15. Remember, the best way to find this out is to know your times tables. I am after a number that, when multiplied by 2 is the closest number I can get to 15 without actually exceeding 15. The number in question is 7:

$$7 \times 2 = 14$$

You can now see that the number 7, when multiplied by 2, is as close as I can get to the number 15 without exceeding it. Therefore, I can now put a number 7 (in bold below) on top of the division sign:

$$
\begin{array}{r}
067 \\
2\overline{)135} \\
\underline{0} \\
13 \\
\underline{12} \\
15 \\
\end{array}
$$

This number 7 can now be multiplied with the 2 outside the division sign to give 14, which will sit under the 15 ready to be subtracted:

$$
\begin{array}{r}
06\!\!\!\text{⃝}7 \\
2\overline{)135} \\
\underline{0} \\
13 \\
\underline{12} \\
15 \\
\underline{14} \\
\end{array}
$$

Subtracting: 15 − 14 = 1

$$
\begin{array}{r}
067 \\
2\overline{)135} \\
\underline{0} \\
13 \\
\underline{12} \\
15 \\
\underline{14} \\
1 \\
\end{array}
$$

I now have yet another remainder of 1. Looking at the division, it appears as if all numbers have been used up and there are no numbers left to bring down to join the 1 on its own. However, the good news is that there are an infinite amount of zeros contained after the last number, which I can bring down to join the number 1 on its own. For clarity of explanation I will show you what I mean (in bold):

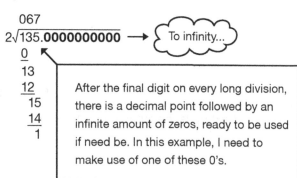

$$
\begin{array}{r}
067 \\
2\overline{)135.\textbf{0000000000}} \longrightarrow \text{To infinity...} \\
\underline{0} \\
13 \\
\underline{12} \\
15 \\
\underline{14} \\
1 \\
\end{array}
$$

After the final digit on every long division, there is a decimal point followed by an infinite amount of zeros, ready to be used if need be. In this example, I need to make use of one of these 0's.

In order to be able to do something with the remainder 1, I will need to bring down a zero to join the 1 because the number 2 does not go into a 1 on its own:

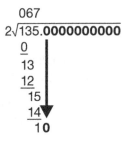

$$
\begin{array}{r}
067 \\
2\sqrt{135.\mathbf{0000000000}} \\
\underline{0} \\
13 \\
\underline{12} \\
15 \\
\underline{14} \\
10
\end{array}
$$

I now ask myself how many times 2 goes into 10. The answer is exactly 5, with no remainders. I can now put a 5 on top of the division sign. However, I need to also put a decimal point after the number 7 on top of the division sign to indicate that this is the point where I 'borrowed' a zero i.e. the point where I brought a zero down to join the 1:

$$
\begin{array}{r}
067.5 \\
2\sqrt{135.0} \\
\underline{0} \\
13 \\
\underline{12} \\
15 \\
\underline{14} \\
10
\end{array}
$$

Now that the 5 is on top of the division sign, I must multiply it by the 2 outside the division sign (circled below) and the answer to the multiplication goes underneath the 10 already there ready to be subtracted:

$$
\begin{array}{r}
067\,\textcircled{5} \\
\textcircled{2}\sqrt{135.0} \\
\underline{0} \\
13 \\
\underline{12} \\
15 \\
\underline{14} \\
10 \\
5 \times 2 = \underline{10}
\end{array}
$$

Next up is the subtraction: 10 − 10 = 0

I have finally got to the point where there are no remainders to deal with. This means the division is now complete:

$$
\begin{array}{r}
067.5 \\
2\overline{)135.0} \\
\underline{0} \\
13 \\
\underline{12} \\
15 \\
\underline{14} \\
10 \\
5\times2=\underline{10} \\
0
\end{array}
$$

The answer to the question is **67.5**

EXAMPLE
This example will show you what to do when dividing by a two digit number.

20 does not go into zero, so I put a zero on top of the division sign and follow the procedure of multiplication then subtraction, which leaves me with 13.

$$
\begin{array}{r}
0 \\
20\overline{)135.0} \\
\underline{0} \\
13
\end{array}
$$

As 20 does not go into the number 1, a zero is placed on top of the division sign, above the number 1 which is currently located inside the division sign, as shown below. The procedure of multiplication and subtraction is then followed which gives me a number 13.

$$
\begin{array}{r}
00 \\
20\overline{)135.0} \\
\underline{0} \\
13 \\
\underline{0} \\
135
\end{array}
$$

20 goes into 135 six times, and so I can now place a 6 on top of the division sign and again carry out the procedure of multiplication and subtraction:

$$20 \times 6 = 120$$

$$135 - 120 = 15$$

I now need to 'borrow' the zero from above. Doing this means that I can make the 15 become a 150, which 20 does go into 7 times.

```
        006
20√135.0
     0   |
    13   |
     0   |
   135   |
   120 ▼
    150
```

I can now put a 7 on top of the division sign and carry out the multiplication and subtraction procedures. However, I need to add a decimal point on top of the division sign before I place the number 7 there:

```
        006
20√135.0
     0   |
    13   |
     0   |
   135   |
   120 ▼
    150
    140
     10
```

Unfortunately, 20 does not go into 10, so I will need to borrow another zero from above (in bold below) so that the 10 becomes 100, which 20 does go into exactly 5 times.

```
       006.7
20√135.00
       0
      13
       0
     135
     120
      150
      140
       100
```

Because 20 goes into 100 five times exactly, I can now place a 5 on top of the division sign and carry out the multiplication and subtraction procedures as normal:

```
       006.75
20√135.00
       0
      13
       0
     135
     120
      150
      140
       100
       100
         0
```

There are no more remainders which means I have arrived at the final answer for this division.

Therefore, 135 ÷ 20 = 6.75

Have a go at the end of chapter practice questions. If you get stuck, consult an above example similar to the question you are stuck on for guidance. The questions are not designed to catch you out or trick you in any shape or form; they are there to boost your problem solving confidence.

END OF CHAPTER PRACTICE QUESTIONS (LONG DIVISION)

1. $60 \div 2$

2. $65 \div 2$

3. $70 \div 4$

4. $15 \div 2$

5. $375 \div 2$

6. $895 \div 2$

7. $455 \div 4$

8. $444 \div 2$

   (Hint: The division is not over until all numbers inside the division sign have been used)

9. $168 \div 15$

10. $295 \div 20$

11. $270 \div 15$

12. $150 \div 20$

13. $5 \div 2$

14. $333 \div 3$

15. $3483 \div 15$

16. $3717 \div 21$

17. $7920 \div 22$

18. $350 \div 10$

19. $480 \div 40$

20. $510 \div 6$

21. $175 \div 2$

22. $175 \div 20$

CHAPTER 5
DIRECTED NUMBERS

Numbers which are negative in value do exist up to negative infinity. These numbers are denoted with a minus sign in front of them e.g. –3.

Positive numbers do not usually have the plus sign displayed in front of them unless the number is part of an equation or formula e.g. $2x + 3$. The 3 has a plus in front to show that it is added to the $2x$ term. So if you see the number 3 on its own with no sign in front, it is safe to assume that it is a positive number.

This chapter will familiarise you with the addition, subtraction, multiplication and division of numbers which involve a combination of negative and positive.

ADDING AND SUBTRACTING

The basic rules for adding and subtracting are:

A plus and a minus make a minus (+) (–) = (–)

A minus and another minus together make a positive (–) (–) = (+)

A plus and a plus make a plus (+) (+) = (+)

EXAMPLE:
Evaluate 5 + (−2)

SOLUTION:
5 + (−2) is exactly the same as 5 − 2 because a plus and a minus make a minus.

Therefore the answer is: 5 + (−2) = 5 − 2 = **3**

EXAMPLE:
Evaluate 5− (−2)

SOLUTION:
5− (−2) is exactly the same as 5+2 because two minuses make a plus.

Therefore the answer is 5 − (−2) = 5 + 2 = **7**

EXAMPLE:

Evaluate 5 + 2

SOLUTION:
Nothing changes as we are dealing with two plus signs together. The question can also be written as:

Evaluate 5 + (+2)

A question is never written in this form simply because it is accepted that if a number does not have a negative sign in front of it, then that number must be a positive one.

The answer to this question is therefore **7**

DIVIDING

The basic rules for dividing are:

If two positive numbers are divided this gives a positive answer $\dfrac{(+)}{(+)} = (+)$

If two negative numbers are divided this gives a positive answer $\dfrac{(-)}{(-)} = (+)$

Negative and positive divided gives a negative answer $\dfrac{(-)}{(+)} = (-)$ or $\dfrac{(+)}{(-)} = (-)$

EXAMPLE

Work out $\dfrac{4}{2}$

SOLUTION

From the rules above, I know that two positive numbers divided give a positive answer i.e. no negative numbers are involved so the answer is:

$$\frac{4}{2} = 2$$

EXAMPLE

Work out $\dfrac{-4}{-2}$

SOLUTION

From the rules above, dividing by two negative numbers gives a positive answer, so I can now treat this question as if the negative signs were never in front of the numbers in the first place. The answer is:

$$\frac{-4}{-2} = 2$$

EXAMPLE

Work out $\dfrac{4}{-2}$

SOLUTION

From the rules above, I know that dividing a positive number by a negative one gives a negative answer:

$$\frac{4}{-2} = -2$$

EXAMPLE

Work out $\dfrac{-4}{2}$

SOLUTION

This is the same question as above. The only difference is that the minus sign is now on the top half of the fraction. This makes no difference to the answer as we are dividing a negative number by a positive number which, according to the rules stated above, give a negative answer:

$$\frac{-4}{2} = -2$$

MULTIPLYING DIRECTED NUMBERS

If two positive numbers are multiplied this gives a positive answer
(+) × (+) = (+)

If two negative numbers are multiplied this gives a positive answer
(−) × (−) = (+)

If negative and positive are multiplied this gives a negative answer
(+) × (−) = (−)

You are strongly advised to learn the above rules as you will need to use them over and over again for maths GCSE. Tips for memorising these rules are given at the end of this chapter.

EXAMPLE
Work out (−5) × (−2)

SOLUTION
From the rules above I know that two negative numbers give a positive answer which means I can 'ignore' the two negative signs and treat this question as if it's asking me to work out 5×2. The answer is therefore:

(−5) × (−2) = (+)**10**

The plus sign seen in front of the 10 above is to demonstrate that the answer is a positive number. In an exam it is not necessary to include the plus sign in front of your answer because the examiners (and all mathematicians) accept that if a number does not have a negative sign in front of it then it is a positive number.

EXAMPLE
Work out 5 × –2

SOLUTION
From the rules given above I know that multiplying a positive number with a negative answer should give me an answer which is negative:

$$5 \times -2 = -\mathbf{10}$$

Note that it is now necessary to put the sign in front of the answer 10 in order to show that the answer is a negative number.

EXAMPLE
Work out 5 × 2

SOLUTION
From the rules above, I know that multiplying two positive numbers together give a positive answer:

$$5 \times 2 = \mathbf{10}$$

TIPS FOR MEMORISING THE RULES IN THIS CHAPTER:

Questions involving all positive numbers are the easy ones because we are only dealing with positives and there are no negatives involved. So when faced with a question involving positives you should remember that the answer will always be positive. Trickier questions involve negative signs. A good way of remembering how to deal with this is to think of a negative sign as dominating. So when you have a plus and a minus together, the minus always wins and so the answer will come out as negative. If you have two minus signs, think of one of the minus signs staying horizontal and the other minus sign being placed vertically on top of the horizontal one to make a plus sign:

⊖ ⟶ ⏀ (This is a minus sign rotated by 90° so that it is now vertical)

Imagine laying this on top of a minus sign used in everyday calculations:

⊖⏀ ⟶ +

This will help you to remember that when faced with two minus signs, the answer is always positive.

DIRECTED NUMBERS: END OF CHAPTER QUESTIONS

Work out the following:

1. $-2 - (-3)$
2. $-4 - (-6)$
3. $-7 - (-8)$
4. $-1 - (-1)$
5. $-3 - (-5)$
6. $-8 - (-0)$
7. $-4 - (-1)$
8. $-16 - (-4)$
9. $-12 - (-18)$
10. $-5 - (-2)$
11. $-1 - (-29)$
12. $-2 - (-100)$
13. $-8 - (-6)$
14. $-7 - (-14)$
15. $-25 - (-25)$
16. $19 + 1$
17. $20 + 1$
18. $22 + 2$
19. $2 + 3$
20. $7 + 8$
21. $16 + 4$
22. $17 + 3$
23. $21 + 22$

24. 5 – (–2)

25. 8 – (–2)

26. 10 – (–10)

27. 20 – (–10)

28. 15 – (–6)

29. 15 + (–6)

30. 20 + (–5)

31. 21 + (–3)

32. 5 + (–1)

33. 9 – (–1)

34. –9 + 1

35. –12 + 2

36. –25 + 5

37. –100 + 100

38. –65 + 2

39. –13 + 3

40. 13 – 3

41. 12 – 2

42. 10 – 2

43. 5 – 2

44. 6 – 8

45. 7 – 21

46. 6 – 18

47. 12 – 18

48. $(-12) \div (-2)$

49. $\dfrac{-12}{2}$

50. $\dfrac{12}{4}$

51. $\dfrac{18}{-3}$

52. $\dfrac{-6}{3}$

53. $\dfrac{-28}{7}$

54. $\dfrac{-12}{3}$

55. $\dfrac{60}{10}$

56. $\dfrac{60}{12}$

57. $\dfrac{14}{-2}$

58. $\dfrac{24}{-6}$

59. -12×1

60. 13×-1

61. 11×-1

62. -12×-12

63. 12×-12

64. 12×12

65. -11×-11

66. 16×-2

67. 10×10

68. -15×-10

69. -14×2

70. 2×-2

CHAPTER 6
LOWEST COMMON MULTIPLE (LCM)

This is the lowest number that two or more numbers will each divide into exactly, without any remainders. The lowest common multiple is often used when adding or subtracting fractions (more commonly known as the lowest common denominator when using fractions) and is also used for solving equations (see the chapters named 'fractions' and 'equations' for examples).

The method for finding the lowest common multiple of any set of numbers is shown below:

EXAMPLE
Find the lowest common multiple (LCM) of 2 and 7:

SOLUTION
I need a number that both 2 and 7 will divide into exactly, without any remainders. To find this, I take the largest number of the two, which is 7 and run through the 7 times table starting right from the beginning i.e. starting at 7 × 1:

7 × 1 = 7 (This is not the LCM as 2 does not divide into 7 exactly)

7 × 2 = 14 (This is the LCM as both 2 and 7 divide into 14 exactly)

The number 14 is divisible by both 2 and 7, and is therefore the lowest common multiple of 2 and 7.

EXAMPLE
Find the lowest common multiple (LCM) of 6 and 9:

SOLUTION
I take the biggest number and work my way up it's times tables, starting at 9 × 1 in this case, until I find a number which divides exactly into both 6 and 9 without any remainders:

9 × 1 = 9 (This is not the LCM as 6 does not divide into 9 exactly)

9 × 2 = 18 (This is the LCM as both 6 and 9 divide into 18 exactly)

Both 6 and 9 divide into 18 without any remainders and so the LCM for 6 and 9 is 18.

EXAMPLE
Find the lowest common multiple (LCM) of 2, 3 and 5:

SOLUTION
I start by taking the largest number, 5 and begin with 5×1, working my way up the 5 times tables until I find a number which 2, 3 and 5 can be divided by exactly without any remainders:

5 × 1 = 5 (This is not the LCM as both 2 and 3 do not divide into 5 exactly)

5 × 2 = 10 (This is not the LCM as 3 does not divide into 10 exactly)

5 × 3 = 15 (This is not the LCM as 2 does not divide into 15 exactly)

5 × 4 = 20 (This is not the LCM as 3 does not divide into 20 exactly)

5 × 5 = 25 (This is not the LCM as both 2 and 3 do not divide into 25 exactly)

5 × 6 = 30 (This is the LCM as all 3 numbers, 2, 3 and 5 divide into 30 exactly, proof below)

30 ÷ 2 = 15

30 ÷ 3 = 10

30 ÷ 5 = 6

So, the lowest common multiple of 2, 3 and 5 is **30**

END OF CHAPTER QUESTIONS (LOWEST COMMON MULTIPLE)

a) 3, 6 and 10

b) 12 and 56

c) 9, 10 and 30

d) 2, 8 and 20

e) 2 and 16

f) 3 and 7

g) 5 and 6

h) 5 and 9

i) 3, 5 and 6

j) 10 and 45

k) 9, 14 and 42

l) 5, 8 and 40

m) 2, 5, 8 and 20

n) 9 and 12

o) 15 and 10

p) 6, 15 and 10

q) 2, 7 and 8

r) 2, 3 and 5

s) 10,16 and 200

CHAPTER 7
FRACTIONS

Fractions are nothing to be afraid of. Once you are confident with long division you will have absolutely no problem working with fractions. This chapter aims to get you familiar with converting fractions into decimals and decimals into fractions. This chapter will also introduce you to multiplying, dividing, adding and subtracting fractions.

You may be required to convert fractions into decimals and the examples below illustrate how to do this without the use of a calculator:

EXAMPLE

Convert $\dfrac{5}{8}$ into a decimal, showing all working out

SOLUTION
This question is basically asking me to divide 8 by 5. I can therefore write this out as a division in the form:

$$8\sqrt{5}$$

You may get confused with which number goes where when trying to write out the division in the above form. If you remember that the largest number in the fraction always remains outside of the division sign, you will never have a problem with this.

I now carry out the division:

8 does not go into 5, which is why there is a zero on top of the division sign. The zero then get's multiplied by the 8 outside the division sign leading to a zero below the 5. This then get's subtracted to leave a 5 beneath the line.

Remember that after the 5 there are hidden zeros which are available to use (in bold below). I borrow one of these zeros to make 50, which 8 does go into:

$$
\begin{array}{r}
0 \\
8\overline{)5.\mathbf{0}} \\
0\downarrow \\
\hline
5\ 0
\end{array}
$$

The question I now ask myself is how many times 8 goes into 50. The answer is 6, because 8×6=48. I can now put a 6 on top of the division sign. Remember that because I borrowed a zero, a decimal place needs to go on top of the division sign before I place the 6 there:

$$
\begin{array}{r}
0 \\
8\overline{)5.0} \\
0\downarrow \\
\hline
5\ 0 \\
4\ 8 \\
\hline
\end{array}
$$

The next calculation to make is:

$$
\begin{array}{r}
-\ 5\ 0 \\
4\ 8 \\
\hline
2
\end{array}
$$

The long division now looks like:

$$
\begin{array}{r}
0.6 \\
8\overline{)5.00} \\
0\downarrow \\
\hline
5\ 0 \\
-\ 4\ 8 \\
\hline
2
\end{array}
$$

I now need to bring down another zero because 8 does not go into 2:

$$
\begin{array}{r}
0.6 \\
8\overline{)5.00} \\
\end{array}
$$

I now have the number 20, which 8 goes into twice because 8×2=16 (remember that I cannot exceed 20, only get as close as possible to it using the number outside the division sign, so multiplying 8 by 2 is the closest I can get to 20 without exceeding it).

I can now put 2 above the division sign to the right of the 6:

$$
\begin{array}{r}
0.6\,2 \\
8\overline{)5.00} \\
\end{array}
$$

8×2=16 goes beneath the 20 to be subtracted. The answer is 4, which means I need to borrow another zero because 8 does not go into 4:

$$
\begin{array}{r}
0.6\,2 \\
8\overline{)5.000} \\
\end{array}
$$

I now have the number 40, which 8 goes into 5 times: 8×5=40. The 5 goes on top of the division sign and the answer of 8×5=40 goes beneath the 40 currently there ready to be subtracted:

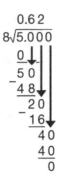

There are no further remainders, which mean that I have reached the end of the division. The answer is 0.625.

Therefore, $\dfrac{5}{8}$ is equal to 0.625

EXAMPLE

Show that the recurring decimal $0.\dot{3}\dot{3} = \dfrac{1}{3}$

SOLUTION

Let $x = 0.\dot{3}\dot{3}$ (the two dots above both 3's mean that the 3's go on forever i.e. 0.333333......)

$100x = 33.333.......$

I can now subtract $100x$ from x, the purpose of doing this is to remove the 0.333..... part so that only the number 33 is left:

$100x - x = 33.333.... -0.333....$

$99x = 33$

$x = \dfrac{33}{99}$

$\dfrac{33}{99}$ can simplify further because 33 goes into 99 exactly 3 times:

$x = \dfrac{33}{99} = \dfrac{1}{3}$

EXAMPLE

Calculate $3\dfrac{3}{8} - 1\dfrac{1}{8}$

SOLUTION

This question involves two parts. The first part is to subtract the whole numbers beside the fractions, which are 3 and 1:

$$3-1=2$$

After the whole numbers have been subtracted, only the fractions remain to be subtracted. I can directly subtract the numerators (top number on a fraction) on both fractions only because the denominators (lower number on a fraction) are the same:

$$\dfrac{3}{8} - \dfrac{1}{8}$$

This is not the final answer as the fraction $\dfrac{2}{8}$ can be further simplified. To simply a fraction, I look at the lowest number, 2, and think about how many times 2 can go into the number 8. The answer is 4, because 4 × 2 = 8. I can now simplify the equation:

$$\dfrac{2}{8} = \dfrac{1}{4}$$

I can now put the whole number, 2, which I calculated at the beginning, beside this simplified fraction to give my final answer of:

$$3\dfrac{3}{8} - 1\dfrac{1}{8} = 2\dfrac{1}{4}$$

EXAMPLE

Calculate $\dfrac{2}{8} + \dfrac{5}{8}$

SOLUTION

Because the denominators are the same, I can add the numerators of the fractions. The final answer is:

$$\dfrac{2}{8} + \dfrac{5}{8} = \dfrac{7}{8}$$

EXAMPLE

a) Calculate $\dfrac{3}{8} \times \dfrac{8}{5}$

b) Calculate $\dfrac{3}{8} \div \dfrac{8}{5}$

c) Calculate $\dfrac{3}{8} \div 2$

SOLUTION

When fractions are multiplied or divided, it does not matter if the denominators are the same.

    a) The main thing I am now looking for in solving this multiplication are two numbers that can cancel each other or simplify.

The two 8's cancel each other (as shown below) to leave:

$$\frac{3}{\cancel{8}} \times \frac{\cancel{8}}{5} = \frac{3}{5}$$

    b) When a question is presented as a division and fractions are involved, the only way to solve the question is to make the question a multiplication of fractions question. This can be done by inverting the fraction which is most on the right (in bold below):

$$\frac{3}{8} \div \frac{\mathbf{8}}{\mathbf{5}} = \frac{3}{8} \times \frac{\mathbf{5}}{\mathbf{8}}$$

This question has now become a multiplication of fractions question and will have the same answer as in section a) of this example as the question is now the same as part a).

    c) When a whole number is given in a multiplication or division of fractions question, then the whole number is actually a disguised fraction. The number 2 can be written as $\dfrac{2}{1}$, which is the whole number 2 written as a fraction. With this in mind, I can now proceed to calculate the answer. I cannot divide fractions and must invert the fraction most to the right so that the question becomes a multiplication of fractions question (inverted fraction shown in bold below):

$$\frac{3}{8} \div \frac{2}{1} = \frac{3}{8} \times \frac{1}{2}$$

$$\frac{3}{8} \times \frac{1}{2} = \frac{3}{16}$$

EXAMPLE

a) Calculate $\dfrac{5}{8} - \dfrac{3}{4}$

b) Calculate $\dfrac{5}{8} + \dfrac{3}{4}$

SOLUTION

a) The denominators of the two fractions are not the same and in order for me to proceed I will need to make them the same. To do this, I focus on the lowest number out of the 2 numbers in the denominator, which is 4 in this case. I now multiply the denominator, 4, by 2 to make it 8:

$$4 \times 2 = 8$$

Because I multiplied the denominator of the 3/4 fraction by 2 to make the denominator 8, I also need to multiply the numerator of the 3/4 fraction by 2:

$$\frac{3}{4} \times \frac{2}{2} = \frac{6}{8}$$

I can now use 6/8 to subtract from 5/8:

$$\frac{5}{8} - \frac{6}{8} = -\frac{1}{8}$$

b) As mentioned in part a), I cannot proceed without making the denominators an equal value. Because I have already done this in part a), I know that 3/4 is the same as 6/8:

$$\frac{5}{8} + \frac{3}{4} = \frac{5}{8} + \frac{6}{8} = \frac{11}{8}$$

The fraction 11/8 can be written with a whole number. This is because 8 goes into 11 once, with a remainder of 3, which means 11/8 can also be written as:

$$\frac{11}{8} = 1\frac{3}{8}$$

Writing the final answer in either form is perfectly acceptable.

END OF CHAPTER QUESTIONS (FRACTIONS)

Where possible, give your answer in the simplest form

1. Show that $0.\dot{2}\dot{7} = \dfrac{3}{11}$

2. Show that $0.\dot{4}\dot{4} = \dfrac{4}{9}$

3. Convert $\dfrac{1}{2}$ into a decimal, showing all working out.

4. Convert $\dfrac{3}{8}$ into a decimal, showing all working out.

5. Convert $\dfrac{3}{4}$ into a decimal, showing all working out.

6. Calculate $\dfrac{3}{8} + \dfrac{2}{5}$

7. Calculate $\dfrac{2}{8} + \dfrac{1}{8}$

8. Calculate $\dfrac{3}{5} + \dfrac{1}{2}$

9. Calculate $2\dfrac{3}{5} - 1\dfrac{1}{2}$

10. Calculate $2\dfrac{3}{5} + 1\dfrac{1}{2}$

11. Write 0.44 as a fraction

12. Calculate $\dfrac{5}{6} + \dfrac{1}{2}$

13. Calculate $\dfrac{5}{6} \div \dfrac{5}{6}$

14. Calculate $\dfrac{3}{8} \div \dfrac{9}{2}$

15. Explain why the statement: '2.5 is the same as $2\dfrac{1}{5}$' is not correct.

16. Calculate $3\dfrac{3}{8} \times 2\dfrac{2}{3}$

17. A train ticket is selling at $\dfrac{1}{6}$ off the normal price of £48, how much is taken off the price of a normal ticket when the discount is applied?

18. Calculate $2\dfrac{1}{8} + 1\dfrac{1}{2}$

19. Place the following fractions in order of size, smallest first:
$$\dfrac{1}{2}, \dfrac{2}{3}, \dfrac{1}{6}, \dfrac{3}{4}$$

20. Calculate
$$3\dfrac{5}{8} \times 2\dfrac{5}{6}$$

CHAPTER 8:
CALCULATING THE MODE, MEDIAN, MEAN, AVERAGE MEAN AND RANGE

This chapter is easy and is about to get even easier for you after we are done with it.

MODE CALCULATIONS

By definition in mathematics, MODE means MOST, the way I remembered this while sitting my exams was to use the link word technique. Ask yourself the following question: 'Which MODE of transport do I use the MOST'. If the answer is a bus, you should think of a bus as a MODE of travel and surprise, automatically you will remember that because you use the bus the MOST it is your MODE of travel. Try it now and in a few days ask yourself what MODE means, you should have no trouble remembering, but if you do have trouble, don't panic, once you start practicing the questions provided in this book, you will become familiar with the concept of calculating the mode.

EXAMPLE
You are working at a shoe factory and your manager requests that you find the most common shoe size out of a sample of 9 pairs of shoes which have the following sizes:

8, 10, 12, 9, 6, 13, 10, 7, 11

What is the most common shoe size?

SOLUTION
Tip: The question asks for the most common shoe size, in other words, the mode. In an exam if you find yourself with this type of question and not a simple 'calculate the mode' type question you should remember the definition of mode given above.

The first thing that needs to be done with every problem involving calculating the mode is to order the numbers, either from lowest to highest or vice versa, it really doesn't matter which of these you choose because we need to see what the most common numbers are. You may be thinking, 'surely I can spot the most frequently occurring number and save time by not having to order the numbers'. You can certainly do this, but why not show the examiner how you arrived at your answer methodically? It won't take that much longer and you will gain extra marks for showing your working out.

So, taking the initial step of reordering the numbers:

6, 7, 8, 9, 10, 10, 11, 12, 13

Note I have chosen to order them from lowest to highest, this is the easiest way of ordering as you can count up as you go along rather than count downwards, which people generally find harder to do mentally.

We can now clearly see that the number 10 occurs twice in the series of shoe sizes, which means it is the most common, which means that 10 is the mode of these particular shoe sizes.

EXAMPLE
Calculate the mode of the following set of numbers:

3, 2, 5, 7, 8, 34, 5, 22

SOLUTION

Rearranging these numbers from lowest to highest we get

2, 3, 5, 5, 7, 8, 22, 34

We can now see that the number which most commonly occurs is the number 5. Therefore the answer for this example is 5.

EXAMPLE
Calculate the mode(s) of the following numbers:

2, 3, 4, 4, 5, 6, 2, 8

SOLUTION
Rearranging the numbers from lowest to highest we get

2, 2, 3, 4, 4, 5, 6, 8

I am now faced with two, different numbers which occur the most. In this case I have two modes, also known as 'bimodal'. Therefore the answer is both 2 and 4.

If you find yourself with a series of numbers which contain more than 2 different numbers this is known as 'multimodal'. The good news is that it would be very rare for a GCSE exam paper to ask you to calculate a multimodal series of numbers, but I have included an example below anyway to make sure you are confident with the topic of modes.

EXAMPLE
Calculate the mode(s) of the following numbers:

3, 5, 2, 4, 5, 5, 3, 3, 4, 4

SOLUTION
Rearranging, as I have always done in previous examples, I get:

2, 3, 3, 3, 4, 4, 4, 5, 5, 5

There are now three different numbers which all occur often; hence the answer to the example is 3, 4 and 5.

The following page gives examples of how to calculate mode when data is in a frequency table.

CALCULATING THE MODE FROM A FREQUENCY TABLE

The definition of mode remains exactly the same and always will remain the same. The only difference now is that I am looking for data which has the highest frequency from a frequency table i.e. data that occurs the most.

EXAMPLE
The table below shows the heights of ceilings in different rooms and the frequency at which they occur. Find the modal interval.

Height (m)	$1 < Y \leq 2$	$2 < Y \leq 3$	$3 < Y \leq 4$	$4 < Y \leq 5$
Frequency	10	6	4	2

Hints: An interval is the term given to all the numbers between and including two numbers. So, for example, if the ceiling height was 2.5m we can say that this height lies in the interval $2 < Y \leq 3$.

SOLUTION
Y in this case represents the height of the ceiling and is a variable within a given interval. The symbol $\leq$ means less than or equal to and the symbol $<$ means less than. So, for example, in the interval $2 < Y \leq 3$ it can be said that Y is less than or equal to 3 and more than 2.

If the directions of the symbols are changed so they are facing the opposite way, it would mean more than, for example $>$ means more than and $\geq$ means more than or equal to.

10 is the highest frequency in the above table and therefore it can be said that

$1 < Y \leq 2$ is the modal interval.

EXAMPLE
Office workers made a collection of the sizes of everyone's shoes in the office out of extreme boredom, calculate the mode:

Shoe size	7	8	9	10
Frequency	2	4	3	1

SOLUTION

The highest frequency is 4 in the above table which means that the most common shoe size in the office is a size 8 i.e. the mode is 8.

MEAN (AVERAGE) CALCULATIONS:

The mean is another term for calculating the average of a set of data. To calculate the mean or average of any set of data add the total of that set of data and divide by how many numbers are in the series:

EXAMPLE

A car travels through an average speed check area with 4 checkpoints and it's speeds (in mph) are recorded as:

30, 31, 35 and 38

Calculate the car's average speed across the average speed check area.

SOLUTION

To tackle this problem you may need a calculator, although I encourage you to avoid using a calculator as much as possible to get practice and give your brain a workout. The steps needed to do this without a calculator are shown below:

To find the average, I must first find the total sum of all numbers in the series added together:

30
+31
+35
+38
134

To add these numbers, first go down the right hand side column so that you are adding 0 + 1 + 5 +8 = 14. However, underneath the line there is only space for one number. For digits such as the 14 produced from the right hand column, it is always the case that the digit furthest to the right is placed here and for the number 14 this is 4, as shown on the left in bold.

Moving onto the left hand column I now add all numbers in this column:

3 + 3 +3 + 3 = 12 +1 = 13

Do not forget that I still have a remainder from the left hand number on the number 14, which is 1, so that now I need to add 1 to 12 which makes 13. As the 4 was previously there, I now have an answer of 134 for the total of the cars average speed.

I now need to calculate an average, this is done by dividing the total by how many numbers there are in the data set, which in this example is 4 as only 4 speeds were recorded for the car travelling through the average speed check:

$$4\sqrt{134}$$

When approached with a division problem, the first thing to do is look at the first number of the number inside the division sign, which in this case is 1. 4 does not go into 1 so I can put a zero on top of the 1. The following colour code will be used for ease explanation and for this division problem only: Numbers in bold are multiplied together and numbers highlighted in black are the result of the multiplication of the two numbers in bold. Also, the result of any subtraction is highlighted in gray. Let's begin:

0
4√134
0

As the zero is on top of the 1, we must multiply the zero by what's outside the division sign (bold). This is standard procedure for any number which is put on top of the division sign.

4 × **0** = 0 , in fact anything multiplied by zero is zero.

The next step is to subtract the bottom number from the top number i.e.1− 0, which leaves the remainder 1, shown below the line (highlighted gray below).

0
4√134
0
1

The next step is to bring down the number 3 to meet the number 1 already beneath the line to make 13.

03
4√134
0↓
13

I now have the number 13, which 4 goes into 3 times with a remainder of 1.

This is because 4 × 3=12 which is what one digit away from 13 is. Because of this, a 3 is placed on top of the division sign.

03
4√134
0↓
13
12
1

As mentioned earlier, the number 3 on top which you now see, is multiplied by the number outside the division sign to give 12.

The bottom number is now subtracted from the top number to give a remainder of 1.

I must now not forget that there is one last number remaining above which is the number 4. Now is the right time to bring the number 4 to meet the remainder just calculated:

Step 4:   03
              4√134
                0↓
                13
                12↓
                14

I now have the number 14. At this point ask yourself how many times 4 goes into 14.

The answer is 3 again.

Continuing, another 3 now goes on top of the division sign. This is then multiplied with the 4 outside the division sign to give 12, which sits underneath the 14 ready to be subtracted:

            033
         4√134
            0↓
            13
            12↓
            14
            12
            2

There is now a remainder of 2 and no numbers left to bring down. In this case and any other case where you are left with a remainder but no numbers to bring down, place a decimal point after the last numbers both in the division sign and out:

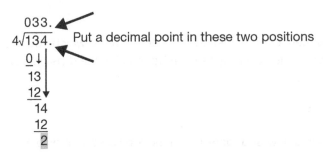

Put a decimal point in these two positions

After a decimal place is put both on top of the division sign and next to the last number within the division sign as shown above, there are an infinite number of zeros which are useful for continuing the calculation. I will need to 'borrow' one of these zero's in order to join the remainder of 2, because 4 does not go into 2. The 2 is currently beneath the line and when the zero is brought down to join it, the number 20 is formed, which the number 4 does go into:

```
    033.
4√134.0
   0↓
  13
  12↓
   14
   12
    2 0
```

I am now faced with the question how many 4s go into 20? The answer is exactly 5 without any remainders. I now need to go through the standard procedure once more and multiply the 5 on top of the division sign by 4 giving 20 (see bold numbers below), which sit's below the last remainder of 20 (highlighted black). Once they are subtracted the remainder is zero and that is my answer.

```
    033.5
4√134.0
   0↓
  13
  12↓
   14
   12
    2 0
    2 0
      0
```

Back to the original question of the car's average speed, the answer is **33.5** mph.

Alternatively, if it is a calculator allowed exam, you could have used a calculator. However, this book will prepare you for all eventualities so that you are prepared to tackle any question in the best way possible, with or without a calculator.

EXAMPLE

Calculate the mean of the following set of data provided:

2, 2, 4, 3, 6, 7, 3, 1, 10, 2

SOLUTION
The first thing to do is to add all the numbers in the set of data, with or without a calculator. It is better to use mental arithmetic so that your brain gets a workout. Use your fingers to count if you have to. You should have got the answer to be 40.

The good thing about doing this without a calculator is that with practice you begin to remember answers to certain combinations such as 5 + 4 = 9 or 7 + 6 = 13 and in no time you should be able to just write down the answer without having to count your fingers.

To calculate the mean, there are 10 numbers in the data set so I divide by 10 in this case:

$$\frac{40}{10} = 4$$

The mean is therefore 4. The above calculation is easily done mentally, simply cancel the two zeros from the top and bottom of the fraction and you are left with:

$$\frac{4}{1} = 4 \text{ (To learn more about these consult the fractions chapter).}$$

CALCULATING THE MEAN (AVERAGE) FROM A FREQUENCY TABLE

The only thing that has changed is that we are now faced with a table rather than a list of numbers. To see what frequency tables actually represent, see the example below:

EXAMPLE
The data set below shows the ages of 6 students in the school canteen. Calculate the mean age of students visiting the canteen:

16, 15, 15, 13, 13, 12

SOLUTION
To find the mean of this set of data, I could add up all the individual ages to give 84 and divide by 6, the amount of student's, to give an average age of 14.

Alternatively, I could also write the above set of data as:

$(16 \times 1) + (15 \times 2) + (13 \times 2) + (12 \times 1) = 84$

The numbers in bold above can also be known as frequencies i.e. how often each age occurs. There is one 16 yr old in the above list and so the frequency of 16 yr olds in the data sample is 1 and for 15 yr olds the frequency is 2 as it is for 13 yr olds and for 12 yr olds the frequency is 1. In a frequency table, this would look like:

Students age	16	15	13	12
Frequency	1	2	2	1

This is the general idea behind frequency tables and the example below gives step by step instructions on how to calculate the mean from a frequency table similar to the one above. This particular frequency table is used in the end of chapter questions (Q7).

EXAMPLE
A rail company monitors the services of its trains over a number of months and the results are shown below. Calculate the mean delay in hours.

Hours of delay	0	1	2	3	4	5
Number of trains	18	12	10	6	3	2

SOLUTION
The first things I need to establish from the first two columns (the boxes with hours of delay and number of trains typed into them in this case)

is which row the variables are in, which I need to calculate the mean of, and which of the two contains frequency . This is straight forward in this example as we know that the row called 'number of trains' is there to show how many trains were delayed i.e. it tells me the frequency or amount of trains which were delayed for a given variable. Since this is the frequency row, the remaining row ('hours of delay') must be the row containing the variables.

Always remember that it's the row containing the variables that we need to find the mean of and not the row containing frequencies. This question instructs you to calculate the mean of the hours of delay, which is the variable and so there is no issue here with which row to calculate the mean of, however in the exam they may not be as nice.

It should be apparent to you, if such a question does appear in the exam as to which row contains the frequency. This is because the first box in the frequency row usually starts with something like 'number of...' or 'amount of....' or wording along those lines etc. For example, the table below has 'number of trains' for its title of the frequency row. It's a giveaway really!

Now I must multiply the two columns together to give a sub total $(x \times y)$:

Hours of delay, x	0	1	2	3	4	5	Total
No. of trains, y	18	12	10	6	3	2	51
$(x \times y)$	0	12	20	18	12	10	72

I must also add all numbers in the number of trains' row, which gives 51 and the $(x \times y)$ row, which gives 72 :

The next step is to calculate the mean, which will be $\frac{72}{51}$ =1.41 which means the mean delay is 1.41 hours. You may use a calculator for such a question as it would be unlikely to see the above division given in a non calculator exam.

This is the procedure for calculating mean from a frequency table, so rehearse this as much as you feel you need to and then try the end of chapter practice questions.

EXAMPLE

The table below shows the heights of ceilings in different rooms and the frequency at which they occur. Find the mean height.

Height (m)	$1 < Y \le 2$	$2 < Y \le 3$	$3 < Y \le 4$	$4 < Y \le 5$
Frequency	10	6	4	2

SOLUTION

With questions such as these with intervals I need to add an extra step compared to the last example. Take the first interval found in the height row, for example, $1 < Y \le 2$, which number would you use to multiply frequency with? 1 or 2....?

The answer is neither

To solve this problem, I must first find the midpoint of the interval. You can do this by either pressing 1 + 2 on a calculator then dividing the answer by 2 or by knowing or calculating that $\frac{3}{2} = 1.5$.

Adding the numbers on each interval and dividing by 2 each time to get the midpoint gives:

Height (m)	$1 < Y \le 2$	$2 < Y \le 3$	$3 < Y \le 4$	$4 < Y \le 5$
Frequency	10	6	4	2
Midpoint	$\frac{1+2}{2} = 1.5$	$\frac{2+3}{2} = 2.5$	$\frac{3+4}{2} = 3.5$	$\frac{4+5}{2} = 4.5$

Now that I have the midpoints, I can treat this as the variable just as I did in the previous example and then multiply this by the frequency.

Height (m)	$1 < Y \le 2$	$2 < Y \le 3$	$3 < Y \le 4$	$4 < Y \le 5$
Frequency	10	6	4	2
Midpoint	1.5	2.5	3.5	4.5
Frequency multiplied by midpoint	$10 \times 1.5 = 15$	$6 \times 2.5 = 15$	$4 \times 3.5 = 14$	$2 \times 4.5 = 9$

The next step is to add up all numbers in the frequency row and find the total of the row and the same should be done with the 'frequency multiplied by midpoint' row:

Height (m)	$1 < Y \le 2$	$2 < Y \le 3$	$3 < Y \le 4$	$4 < Y \le 5$	Total
Frequency	10	6	4	2	22
Midpoint	1.5	2.5	3.5	4.5	
Frequency multiplied by midpoint	15	15	14	9	53

Note that I have omitted the total for midpoint as this is not a necessary step in my calculation of the mean.

I now use these two totals to find the mean:

Mean $= \dfrac{53}{22}$

  $= 2.41$ metres to two decimal places

Therefore, the average height is 2.41 m

On your calculator, type in 53 divided by 22 and you should get 2.40909090909......

I have chosen to 'cut' this long number after the first zero that appears and before the first 9 that appears. This 'cut' takes place two numbers after the decimal place hence why in mathematics we say 'to two decimal places'. However, because I chose to 'cut' the long number before a 9 it means that the number before gets rounded up to a 1 because it is currently zero. If there were a 5, 6, 7 or 8 in place of the 9 this would still be the case. However, if there were a 0,1,2,3 or 4 in place of the 9 then the preceding zero get's left as it is.

MOVING AVERAGES

Moving averages are used to calculate the average of a set of data over a period of time e.g. minutes, hours, weeks, months, years etc. The reason for doing this is because a set of data may be subject to changes over periods of time. For example, sales of jackets in the UK decrease during the summer months compared to the winter months. If a graph were drawn to show this relationship it would have one peak and one trough in every year.

Moving averages level out the large seasonal variations (peaks and troughs) caused by a scenario such as the one described above. By calculating moving averages, slowly changing trends can be detected in the data over a period of time. The examples below will aid your understanding of this topic further.

EXAMPLE
The table gives information about the cost of travel for one family.

Month	Jan-Mar 2009	Apr-Jun 2009	Jul-Sep 2009	Oct-Dec 2009	Jan-Mar 2010	Apr-Jun 2010	Jul-Sep 2010
Cost of travel (in £)	150	75	36	147	162	79	53

a) Work out the four-point moving averages for this information

b) Use your answer to a) to describe the trend

SOLUTION
a) To work out a four point moving average, I start with the first four numbers: 150, 75, 36 and 115.

I need to find the average of these four numbers:

$$\frac{£150 + £75 + £36 + £147}{4} = £102$$

I now **move** one number to the right and calculate the average of the next four numbers, which are 75, 36, 147 and 162:

$$\frac{£75 + £36 + £147 + £162}{4} = £105$$

I again **move** one number to the right again and calculate the average of the next four numbers which are 36, 147, 162 and 79:

$$\frac{£36 + £147 + £162 + £79}{4} = £106$$

Finally, I **move** one number to the right once more and calculate the average of the next four numbers which are 147, 162, 66 and 53:

$$\frac{£147 + £162 + £66 + £53}{4} = £107$$

To summarise, the four point moving averages are:

£102, £105, £106 and £107

b) The trend is that the cost of travel increases with time.

MEDIAN CALCULATIONS

Median, in mathematics, means 'the middle'. A good way of remembering this, one which I used when sitting my exams, is that Italy is in the middle of the med (Mediterranean) sea. To use this example please consult a world map so that you can picture Italy in relation to the Mediterranean Sea. This will significantly improve your chances of remembering the definition of median for your exams and beyond. Alternatively, feel free to let your imagination run wild and come up with your own examples which may be easier for you to remember.

EXAMPLE:
Calculate the median for the following set of numbers:

16, 25, 18, 43, 89, 101, 76

As always with calculations like these, I must order the numbers. I prefer to do this from lowest to highest although it is possible to order them from highest to lowest also.

After ordering the numbers I have:

16, 18, 25, 43, 76, 89, 101

I have 7 numbers above, (it is irrelevant that they are all different numbers because I'm not asked to calculate the mode for this example).

So how do I find which number is in the middle?. The trick to this is to take the number 7 (as I have 7 numbers in the question) and find the next number down from 7 which is divisible by 2.

The next number down from the number 7 which is divisible by 2 is the number 6. As I have established this I can now divide 6 by 2:

$\frac{6}{3}$=2 Note that this can also be written in the form $6 \div 2 = 3$. If you are not familiar with division or fractions, please consult chapter 7 which will familiarise you with it.

I end up with the number 3. The significance of the number 3 is that it tells you how many numbers you can pull aside from each end of the above series of numbers leaving the number 43 on its own as shown below.

Therefore the median is 43

16, 18, 25   **43**   76, 89, 101

EXAMPLE:
A restaurant did a survey on its food quality, 1 is the lowest rating, 10 is the highest. Here are samples of 8 answers to the survey, find the median:

1, 3, 3, 5, 6, 8, 2, 5

SOLUTION
Once again ignoring the fact that the above series of numbers contain more than one of the same number i.e. two 3s and two 5s, I now must order the numbers:

1, 2, 3, 3, 5, 5, 6, 8

In the previous example, the series of numbers contained 7 numbers and 7 is an odd number. However, this example contains 8 numbers and 8 is an even number which is divisible by 2.

This is great news as I can omit the step of finding the next number down to find the number divisible by 2 as in example 1.

Continuing, I must now divide 8 by 2:

$$\frac{8}{2} \quad or \ 8 \div 2 = 4$$

The number 4 now means that there are 4 numbers which can form 2 separate entities:

(1, 2, 3, 3) and (5, 5, 6, 8)

This is not good as now there is no middle number. The way to go about solving the median now is to take the two closest numbers at the separation point and find their average (mean):

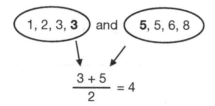

$$\frac{3 + 5}{2} = 4$$

Therefore, the median is 4 for this example

CONCLUDING REMARKS FOR FINDING THE MEDIAN:

If the amount of numbers in the question turns out to be odd then remember to go down to the next even number and divide that by 2. The number which results from the division tells you how many numbers to pull away from the series from both the front and end of it and you will be left with a number in the middle which is the median. For even numbers, divide by 2, then separate the two bunches of numbers and then calculate the mean of the two numbers which are closest to the separation. The result will be the median.

CALCULATING MEDIAN FROM A FREQUENCY TABLE

The definition of median remains the same and I would still need to find the middle value. However, the process of finding this middle value becomes slightly trickier with the addition of a frequency table. This should not worry you as I have made this topic easy for you to understand through examples:

EXAMPLE

Find the median interval height

Height (m)	$1 < Y \leq 2$	$2 < Y \leq 3$	$3 < Y \leq 4$	$4 < Y \leq 5$
Frequency	10	6	4	2

The first thing to do with a question that asks you to calculate the median from this type of frequency table is to add all the frequencies and find a total, 22 in this case and halve this:

$$\frac{22}{2} = 11$$

Height (m)	$1 < Y \leq 2$	$2 < Y \leq 3$	$3 < Y \leq 4$	$4 < Y \leq 5$	Half the total of frequency row
Frequency	10	6	4	2	**11**

The next thing to do is to calculate the cumulative frequency. So the first frequency the table has is 10, and the next is 6 so together the frequency is $10 + 6 = 16$, and then it will be $16 + 4 = 20$ and finally $20 + 2 = 22$:

Height (m)	$1 < Y \leq 2$	$2 < Y \leq 3$	$3 < Y \leq 4$	$4 < Y \leq 5$
Frequency	10	6	4	2
Cumulative Frequency	10	**16**	20	22

The next step is to refer back to number 11, half the total of the frequency row and look for the next number up from 11 on the cumulative frequency row.

So in this case, the next number up from 11 is 16 and as 16, located in the cumulative frequency row, corresponds to the interval $2 < Y \leq 3$ this is the median interval.

EXAMPLE

Calculate the median of the delays to the train services.

Hours of delay	0	1	2	3	4	5
Number of trains	18	12	10	6	3	2

SOLUTION

The method of tackling this is very similar to the previous example. Firstly, work out the total frequency which is the total number of trains in this case by adding the whole row:

Hours of delay	0	1	2	3	4	5	Total
Number of trains	18	12	10	6	3	2	51

As in the previous example, halve this total:

$$\frac{51}{2} = 25.5$$

I will need to remember this result for later.

Next, I calculate the cumulative frequency (note the importance of realising which row is the variable and which is the frequency in order to do this):

Hours of delay	0	1	2	3	4	5	Total
Number of trains	18	12	10	6	3	2	51
Cumulative Frequency	18	30	40	46	49	51	

Now I refer back to halve the total of all frequencies calculated earlier, which is 25.5. I can now ask myself which number is next above 25.5 in the cumulative frequency row. The answer is 30 and this corresponds to a delay of 1 hour. Therefore the median delay is 1 hour.

RANGE CALCULATIONS

The range, in mathematics, is defined as the highest value in the data minus the lowest value.

EXAMPLE

Find the range of the following data:

25, 15, 10, 43, 22, 29, 28, 2, 5, 8, 4, 100, 20, 1

The most logical thing to do in this case, considering I need to establish the highest and lowest values in the data, would be to order them from lowest to highest or vice versa, it's the two numbers at the front and end of the data series that I am interested in (highlighted in black below). This would also show the examiner that you have followed a logical structure to solving the problem and you stand to gain easy extra marks:

1, 2, 4, 5, 8, 10, 15, 20, 22, 25, 28, 29, 43, 100

The range is given by the subtraction of the highest data value from the lowest, which is:

$$100 - 1 = 99$$

The range for this example is therefore **99**.

This process can be repeated for any data series you find yourself faced with.

EXAMPLE

The table below shows the cost of using the train to travel certain distances and how often people use it, determine the range for this set of data:

COST	FREQUENCY
1	15
5	6
7	4
4	9

The range in this case is simply determined by subtracting the highest cost from the lowest cost, giving a range of 7 − 1 = **6**

A range calculation question given in an exam should be considered a gift as it is so simple.

This concludes the chapter. At this point you should be well prepared to tackle all mode, median, mean, moving average and range questions. It is important that you try ALL the end of chapter questions provided until you feel completely confident with these topics.

END OF CHAPTER QUESTIONS (CALCULATING THE MODE, MEDIAN, MEAN, MOVING AVERAGES AND RANGE)

1. John made a list of times, in minutes, taken to cook 50 different meals. The following table shows information on these times:

Time, (t minutes)	Frequency
$0 < t \leq 5$	10
$0 < t \leq 10$	16
$0 < t \leq 15$	13
$0 < t \leq 20$	8
$0 < t \leq 25$	3

Calculate/ find:
   i) The mean time taken to cook each meal
   ii) The median interval
   iii) The modal interval

2. For the following 7 numbers, calculate the median: 22, 5, 8, 7, 3, 2, 9

3. Calculate the median of the delays to the train services.

Hours of delay	0	1	2	3	4	5
Number of trains	18	12	10	6	3	2

4. Find the median interval height

Height (m)	$1 < Y \leq 2$	$2 < Y \leq 3$	$3 < Y \leq 4$	$4 < Y \leq 5$
Frequency	10	6	4	2

5. The table below shows the number of students who are late each term.

	2009			2010		
	1st term	2nd term	3rd term	1st term	2nd term	3rd term
Number of late students	25	48	32	28	60	63

The first 3-point moving average is 35. Calculate the second and third 3-point moving averages and describe the trend.

6. A rail company monitors the services of its trains over a number of months and the results are shown below. Calculate the mean delay in hours.

Hours of delay	0	1	2	3	4	5
Number of trains	21	16	12	8	6	3

7. The data set below shows the ages of 6 students in the school canteen. Calculate the mean age of students visiting the canteen:

Students age	16	15	13	12
Frequency	1	2	2	1

CHAPTER 9:
CUMULATIVE FREQUENCY GRAPHS

Following on from the above chapter, you may be asked to plot a cumulative frequency graph in the exam and then calculate the median from the graph. The procedure for doing this is given below.

EXAMPLE

A company which specialises in car repairs does a survey on the amount of money spent on repairs by 120 car owners throughout the year.

The cumulative frequency table below displays the results:

Amount spent (£x)	Cumulative frequency
$0 \leq x < 100$	13
$0 \leq x < 150$	25
$0 \leq x < 200$	42
$0 \leq x < 250$	64
$0 \leq x < 300$	93
$0 \leq x < 350$	110
$0 \leq x < 400$	120

a) Construct a cumulative frequency diagram on the grid provided below

b) Using the cumulative frequency diagram, estimate the median

c) Using the same graph, estimate the lower and upper quartiles.

d) Write down the interquartile range.

SOLUTION

a) When asked to plot a cumulative frequency graph, always plot the points on the right hand side of the interval, which should be the highest value along with the cumulative frequency. For this example, the points to plot on the graph are:

(0, 0), (100, 13), (150, 25), (200, 42), (250, 64), (300, 93), (350, 110) and (400,120)

Note that although the point (0, 0) is not shown on the table, it is still always plotted. Once plotted (see below), the graph will give information such as how many car owners spent less than or equal to a certain amount.

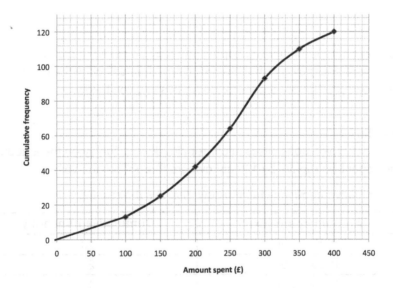

b) To estimate the median, I need data that has been ordered in terms of size and by plotting the cumulative frequency graph above, I have already ordered the data in terms of size. I now need to pick the 'middle' value, which is the definition of median.

The procedure for finding the median in this situation is to halve the 120 car owners who took part in the survey. Half of 120 is 60, so I now need to go along horizontally from 60 on the y axis until I hit the curve then move vertically down to the x axis as shown below:

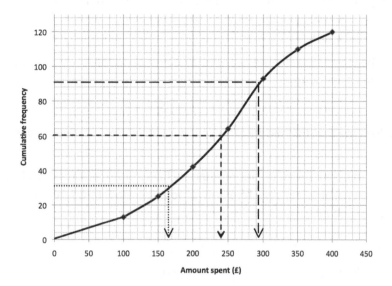

Where the line hits the 'amount spent' axis is the median, which is 240 for this example.

c) To estimate the lower quartile, I need to calculate 25% of the total amount of car owners i.e. 25% of 120.

In mathematics, 'of' means multiply, so to work out 25% **of** 120 I do the following calculation (If you find you are having trouble with these fractions it may be worth revisiting the fractions chapter):

$$\frac{25}{100} \times 120 = \frac{1}{4} \times 120 = 30$$

This means I go horizontally along from 30 and when I hit the curve I go downwards towards the x axis (dotted lines on the above graph), the dotted line hits the x axis at 165, so the lower quartile is 165.

To estimate the upper quartile, I need to calculate 75% of 120:

$$\frac{75}{100} \times 120 = \frac{3}{4} \times 120 = 90$$

I now go horizontally from 90 on the y axis until I reach the curve. I then go vertically downwards until I hit the x axis (purple lines above). The purple line hits the x axis at 295 which means the upper quartile is 295.

d) The interquartile range is found by subtracting the lower quartile from the upper quartile:

Upper quartile – Lower quartile = 295 – 165 = 130

This tells me that the middle 50% of the survey differ in amount spent by £130.

With all this data (median, upper quartile, lower quartile, lowest and highest y axis values), it is possible to create a box plot. How to do this is explained in the next chapter.

END OF CHAPTER QUESTIONS (CUMULATIVE FREQUENCY GRAPHS)

1. Cinema A did a survey on the amount spent by 100 visitors on cinema tickets and popcorn over the period of a year.

   The table below gives information about the amount spent by the 100 visitors to cinema A:

Amount spent (£x)	Cumulative frequency
$0 \leq x < 20$	4
$0 \leq x < 40$	10
$0 \leq x < 60$	14
$0 \leq x < 80$	22
$0 \leq x < 100$	66
$0 \leq x < 120$	102
$0 \leq x < 140$	114
$0 \leq x < 160$	120

a) On the grid below, construct a cumulative frequency graph for this data

b) Use the graph to find an estimate for the median

Another survey from a different cinema, cinema B, gave a median of £115 when 120 people were surveyed.

c) Which cinema's visitors, on average, spent the most throughout the year? State how you arrived at your answer.

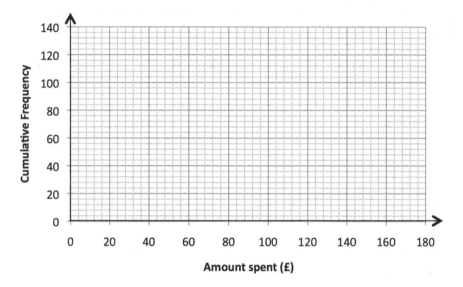

2. 100 students took part in a maths challenge, information on the time it took each student to complete the challenge is given below:

Time (t seconds)	Frequency
$0 < t \le 5$	9
$5 < t \le 10$	20
$10 < t \le 15$	33
$15 < t \le 20$	25
$20 < t \le 25$	13

a) In the table below, complete the cumulative frequency column

Time (t seconds)	Cumulative frequency
$0 < t \le 5$	9
$5 < t \le 10$	
$10 < t \le 15$	
$15 < t \le 20$	
$20 < t \le 25$	

b) Construct a cumulative frequency graph using the grid below to show this information.

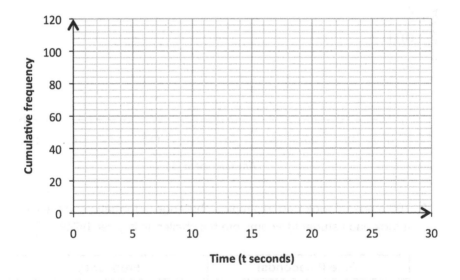

c) From the graph, how many students took more than 10 seconds to finish the maths challenge?

CHAPTER 10:
BOX AND WHISKER PLOTS (OR BOX PLOTS)

Box and whisker plots are useful as they say several things about a set of data in one diagram such as:

- Median of the data

- Range of the data

- Negative and positive skew

The main use of box and whisker plots is that they show the spread of data i.e. it is easy to see where most of the numbers are.

EXAMPLE
Construct a box-plot for the following 13 numbers:

12, 10, 8, 16, 9, 5, 6, 8, 13, 15, 12, 11, 10, 20

SOLUTION
To construct a box plot, the first thing I need to do is to order the numbers so that I can easily find the median:

5, 6, 8, 8, 9 10, 10, 11, 12, 13, 15, 16, 20

To find the median:

Because I have 13 numbers and 13 is odd, I subtract 1 and divide by 2 to find where the median is:

$$\frac{13 - 1}{2} = 6$$

The number 6 means I can separate the first 6 numbers from the left and the last 6 numbers from the right to leave the median (circled below):

5, 6, 8, 8, 9 10, (10) 11, 12, 13, 15, 16, 20

Next I need to find what is termed as 'the lower median'. This is the median of the first 6 numbers:

6 is an even number, so the median will be:

$$\frac{6 + 1}{2} = 3.5 \text{ digits in from the left hand side}$$

5, 6, 8, ⋮ 8, 9 10

This places the lower median between the two 8's, which makes the lower median:

$$\frac{8 + 8}{2} = 8$$

Next I need to find an upper median which is the median of the last 6 numbers. I know from previously that the median is 3.5 digits in and this is where the dotted line goes to indicate the upper median is there

11, 12, 13, ⋮ 15, 16, 20

To find the upper median, I need to take an average of the two numbers, 13 and 15 which are either side of the dotted line:

$$\frac{13 + 15}{2} = 14$$

Therefore, the upper median is 14.

The box plot is ready to be constructed and needs to be started by drawing a number line which can contain all 13 numbers above. Once this is done, I mark lines above where the median (10), lower median (8) and upper median (14) belong as shown below:

I can now create a box using the upper and lower median as endpoints of the box:

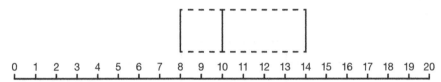

Next, I need to create what are known as 'the whiskers' for the box. This can easily be done by extending a line from both ends of the boxes to the highest (20) and lowest (5) values:

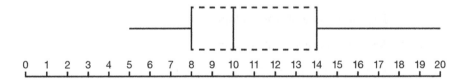

And that is how to create a box and whisker plot. The whisker to the right of the box is longer than the whisker on the left of the box and this means that the data is positively skewed.

If the whisker to the left of the box had been longer than the right, then I could say that the distribution is negatively skewed, but in this instance it is not. A box plot can give you the interquartile range of the data, the range, the median and the max and min values:

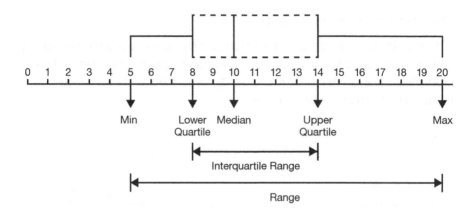

END OF CHAPTER QUESTIONS (BOX PLOTS)

1.

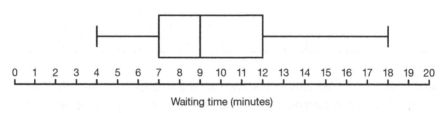

Waiting time (minutes)

The box plot above gives information about the waiting times, in minutes, for the bus.

a) Write down the greatest waiting time.

b) Write down the median waiting time.

c) Work out the interquartile range of the waiting time.

2. For the following set of data:

4, 3, 9, 10, 16, 20, 15, 11, 12, 8, 18, 17, 6

a) Calculate the median

b) Calculate the upper and lower quartiles

c) Write down the smallest and largest numbers in the data

d) Create a box and whisker diagram for the above set of data

CHAPTER 11:
HISTOGRAMS

Although histograms look like bar charts, they are different because the heights of the bars in a bar chart represent frequency whereas for histograms the area of the bars, which can vary, represent frequency. The y-axis of a histogram is labelled as 'frequency density'. Frequency density is the frequency of a particular group divided by the width of that group:

$$\textit{Frequency density} = \frac{\textit{frequency}}{\textit{width of group}}$$

Rearranging this formula gives an expression for calculating the frequency:

$$\textit{Frequency} = \textit{Frequency density} \times \textit{width of group}$$

In the exam, you may be asked to complete a frequency table using information from a histogram or you could be given a table with frequencies and asked to construct a histogram.

EXAMPLE
The histogram below shows the speed, in mph, of 170 cars along a motorway.

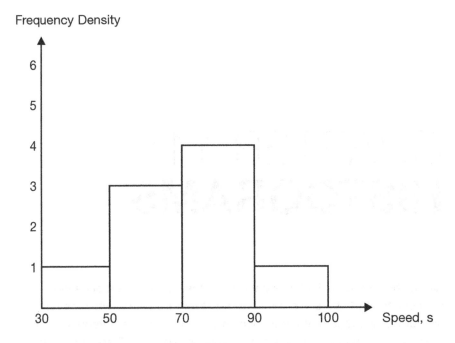

Frequency Density

Speed, s

Using the above histogram, complete the frequency column in the table below

Speed, (mph)	Frequency
$30 \leq s < 50$	
$50 \leq s < 70$	
$70 \leq s < 90$	
$90 \leq s < 100$	

SOLUTION

To complete the frequency column in the table above, I will need to calculate the area of each bar in the histogram individually as the answers for the area of each bar will be the frequency for that particular group.

I begin by calculating the frequency of the $30 \leq s < 50$ group:

The group width is $50 - 30 = 20$. I now multiply this by the frequency density, which is 1:

Frequency = Frequency density x width of group

Frequency = 20 × 1 = 20

The frequency of the 30 ≤ s < 50 group is 20. I now repeat this process for all groups:

Frequency of the group 50 ≤ s < 70 is:

20 × 3 = 60

Frequency of the group 70 ≤ s < 90 is:

20 × 4 = 80

Frequency of the group 90 ≤ s < 100 is:

10 × 1 = 10

I am now able to complete the table:

Speed, (mph)	Frequency
30 ≤ s < 50	20
50 ≤ s < 70	60
70 ≤ s < 90	80
90 ≤ s < 100	10

EXAMPLE
A race takes place with 52 cyclists. Information about the time taken, in minutes, to complete the race is given below.

Time taken (x) minutes	Frequency
0 < x ≤ 5	3
5 < x ≤ 10	8
10 < x ≤ 20	20
20 < x ≤ 40	16
40 < x ≤ 45	5

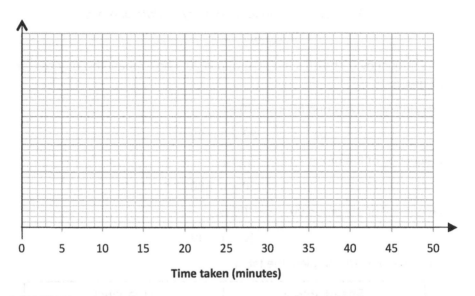

Time taken (minutes)

SOLUTION

In order for me to construct a histogram from the above information, I will firstly need to calculate the frequency density for each group. To do this, I use the formula:

$$Frequency\ density = \frac{frequency}{width\ of\ group}$$

I start with the first group:

Frequency density for $0 < x \le 5$:

The width of this group is 5, because $5 - 0 = 5$ and the frequency is 3 (from the table). I can now use the formula for frequency density:

$$Frequency\ density = \frac{3}{5} = 0.6$$

Following the same procedure for the rest of the groups, I get:

Frequency density for $5 < x \le 10$:

$$Frequency\ density = \frac{8}{5} = 1.6$$

Frequency density for $10 < x \le 20$

$$Frequency\ density = \frac{20}{10} = 2$$

Frequency density for $20 < x \le 40$

$$Frequency\ density = \frac{16}{20} = 0.8$$

Frequency density for $40 < x \le 45$

$$Frequency\ density = \frac{5}{5} = 1$$

Now that I have all the frequency densities, I can construct the histogram:

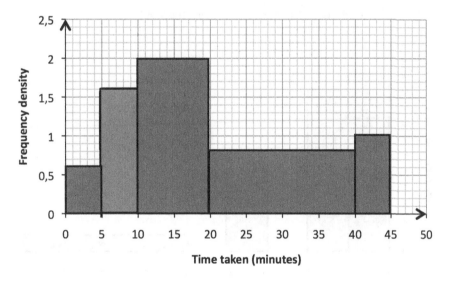

END OF CHAPTER PRACTICE QUESTIONS
(HISTOGRAMS)

1. The table and histogram below both give information on the time taken, in hours, by 210 aircraft to arrive at their final destination after takeoff.

Time (t hours)	Frequency
$0 < t \le 5$	55
$5 < t \le 10$	
$10 < t \le 15$	60
$15 < t \le 20$	
$20 < t \le 25$	25
$25 < t \le 45$	

a) Use the histogram to complete the above table

b) Use the table to complete the histogram below

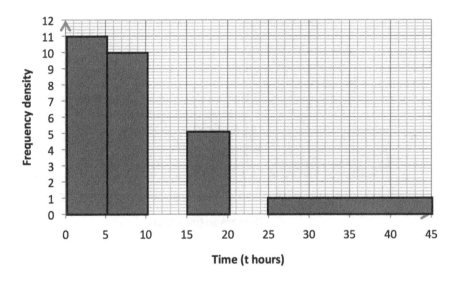

CHAPTER 12:
FREQUENCY POLYGONS

Frequency polygons can be used to represent data that is in a group. In the exam you may be given grouped data in a table with their corresponding frequencies and asked to draw a frequency polygon.

EXAMPLE

A race takes place with 52 cyclists. Information about the time taken, in minutes, to complete the race is given below.

Time taken (x) minutes	Frequency
$0 < x \leq 5$	3
$5 < x \leq 10$	8
$10 < x \leq 20$	20
$20 < x \leq 40$	16
$40 < x \leq 45$	5

Draw a frequency polygon on the grid below for this information.

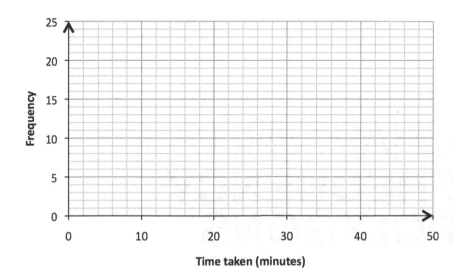

SOLUTION

A frequency polygon can be plotted once the average of each group is calculated. The first group in the table is $0 < x \leq 5$ and the average of this group is:

$$\frac{0 + 5}{2} = \frac{5}{2} = 2.5$$

I now plot the point (2.5, 3) on the graph (gray cross below).

The average of the next group, $5 < x \leq 10$ is:

$$\frac{5 + 10}{2} = 7.5$$

I now plot the point (7.5, 8) on the graph. This process continues until the midpoints of all groups are calculated and then plotted with their corresponding frequency.

To get the graph seen below, I plotted the following points:

(2.5, 3), (7.5, 8), (15, 20), (30, 16) and (42.5, 5)

Once the points are plotted, they can be joined using straight lines as seen below (black line).

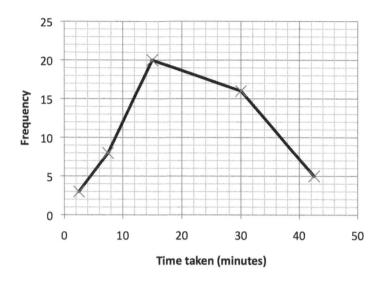

Time taken (minutes)

END OF CHAPTER QUESTIONS (FREQUENCY POLYGONS)

1. 65 people take their driving theory test. Information about the times taken, in minutes, to complete the theory test is given below.

Time taken (x) minutes	Frequency
$0 < x \le 5$	7
$5 < x \le 10$	11
$10 < x \le 20$	25
$20 < x \le 40$	13
$40 < x \le 45$	9

Draw a frequency polygon on the grid below to display this information

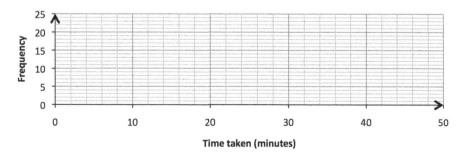

Time taken (minutes)

CHAPTER 13:
STEM AND LEAF DIAGRAMS

Stem and leaf diagrams are another way of storing large amounts of data in an organised way.

The name stem and leaf is used to describe how digits are separated. For two digit numbers, the tens are separated from the units.

For example, the number 15 is broken up into a 1 and a 5. The first digit is known as the stem and the second as the leaf:

Given a large list of numbers, this becomes useful as I can write all the list of numbers in a stem and leaf diagram. This enables me to see the distribution of the data and easily identify any trends in the data. For example:

Students in class B1 sit their mock exams; the results are given below out of 100.

Stem	Leaf
9	1 2 4 6 8 9
8	1 2
7	7 8
6	6
5	0

Key
9 | 0 = 90

Straight away, I can tell that the majority of the students scored above 90% as the stem 9 contains the most leaves. I can also see that one student scored exactly 50% and another scored 66%. Altogether, if I count the amount of leaves in the right hand side of the table it totals 12. This means that 12 students sat the mock exam.

EXAMPLE
Here are the finishing times, in seconds, of 15 sprinters who took part in a race.

18   28   24   22   26

21   43   18   56   42

52   20   33   39   29

a) Draw an ordered stem and leaf diagram showing the information above. Include a key in your answer.

b) What is the range of the finishing times?

c) What is the median of the finishing times?

d) What are the upper and lower quartiles for these times?

e) What is the mode of the finishing times?

SOLUTION

The first thing I need to do is to order the numbers from lowest to highest:

18, 18, 20, 21, 22, 24, 26, 28, 29, 33, 39, 42, 43, 52, 56

a) Using the key: 2 | 0 = 20 I can now put the numbers into an ordered stem and leaf diagram:

Stem	Leaf
1	8 8
2	0 1 2 4 6 8 9
3	3 9
4	2 3
5	2 6

Key
2 | 0 = 20

b) The range of the finishing times is given by the last sprinter's time to finish the race minus the first sprinter's time to finish the race:

Range = 56 – 18 = 38

c) There are 15 finishing times. Because 15 is an odd number, I need to use the rules explained in the 'median' chapter, which will give me the number on which the median lies:

$$\frac{15 + 1}{2} = 8$$

This means the median is on the 8th number in the stem and leaf diagram, which happens to be a number 28 (in bold below). I can check this is correct by counting the numbers either side of the 8th number, there should be equal numbers on both sides.

Stem	Leaf
1	8 8
2	0 1 2 4 6 **8** 9
3	3 9
4	2 3
5	2 6

Count the number of 'leaves' to the left of the number 28 in bold and then count the number of 'leaves' to the right of the number 28 in bold, not including 28 itself. You should find that there are 7 numbers either side of the 28 in bold. This is a check to see that this is the median.

Therefore, the median of the finishing times is 28

d) The upper quartiles and lower quartiles, put simply, are the median of the upper and lower half of the data. I will need to find the medians of the upper and lower half of the data to find the answer to this part of the question. The numbers in the lower half are in italic (lower because the numbers are lowest here) and the numbers in the upper half are in bold italic below:

Stem	Leaf
1	*8 8*
2	*0 1 2 4 6* **8 9**
3	**3 9**
4	**2 3**
5	**2 6**

To find the median of the lower half (numbers in italic):

I know that there are 7 numbers in italic, which is an odd number. From the median chapter, the rule is add 1 and divide by 2, $\frac{7+1}{2} = 4$

Therefore, the 4th number from either the first finishing time or to the left of the 28 in bold above is the lower quartile. The 4th number from either end is the number 21.

To find the median of the upper half (numbers in bold italic), the same applies, because there are 7 numbers in bold italic. Therefore, the 4th number in from either the last finishing time or 4th number to the right of the 28 in bold is the upper quartile. The 4th number from either side is the number 42.

For clarity, the lower quartile, 21, and the upper quartile, 42 are highlighted in black below:

Stem		Leaf						
1	8	8						
2	0	**1**	2	4	6	**8**	**9**	
3	**3**	**9**						
4	**2**	**3**						
5	2	6						

e) The mode is the finishing time which appears the most often in the above data. Two sprinters both crossed the finish line at 18 seconds. There are no other times where two or more sprinters crossed the line together. Therefore, the mode is 18 seconds.

END OF CHAPTER QUESTIONS (STEM AND LEAF DIAGRAMS)

Here are the finishing times, in seconds, of 25 sprinters who took part in a race.

$$\begin{array}{ccccc} 16 & 22 & 21 & 28 & 31 \\ 20 & 45 & 15 & 52 & 47 \\ 42 & 25 & 34 & 39 & 29 \\ 55 & 18 & 23 & 27 & 36 \\ 19 & 33 & 43 & 52 & 17 \end{array}$$

a) Draw an ordered stem and leaf diagram showing the information above. Include a key in your answer.

b) What is the range of the finishing times?

c) What is the median of the finishing times?

d) What are the upper and lower quartiles for these times?

e) What is the mode of the finishing times?

CHAPTER 14:
RATIOS

This chapter will help you to solve exam type problems involving ratios.

A good way of understanding what ratios represent is to imagine 4 items, let's say 4 sweets, 3 of which are red in colour and the remaining sweet is blue. The ratio of the red sweets to the blue sweet can be written as:

Ratio red to blue 3:1

In simple terms, this means that for every 3 red sweets there is 1 blue sweet.

EXAMPLE
In a box, there are:

21 red sweets
14 blue sweets

Write down the ratio of the number of red sweets to the number of blue sweets. Give your ratio in its simplest form.

SOLUTION
I can write the ratio as:

Ratio red to blue 21:14

However, this is not the final answer as the ratio is not in its simplest form yet. In order for me to get this ratio into its simplest form I will need to temporarily treat it as a fraction:

The ratio 21:14 can now be written as the fraction $\frac{21}{14}$

I now simplify the fraction $\frac{21}{14}$:

$$\frac{21}{14} = 1\frac{7}{14} = 1\frac{1}{2} = \frac{3}{2}$$

This means that the ratio 21:14 is the same as the ratio 3:2, which is the simplest form.

Ratios can also be used to find how many item's are in a box for example. How to do this is shown below.

EXAMPLE
There are red and blue sweets in a box.
The total number of red and blue sweets is 44.
The ratio of the number of red sweets to the number of blue sweets is 1:3
Work out the number of blue sweets in the box

SOLUTION
If you understand and memorise the procedure below, you should not have trouble answering these types of ratio questions in the exam.

The first thing to do here is to look at the ratio 1:3. I add the two numbers so that I can divide this by the total amount of sweets in the box 1 + 3 = 4

The total number of red and blue sweets is 44. I now divide 44 by 4:

$$44÷4=11$$

To find the number of blue sweets in the box, I use the number **3** from the ratio 1:**3** and multiply this by 11:

$$11 × 3 = 33 \text{ Blue sweets in the box.}$$

The next example shows how to proceed with a ratio involving 3 numbers rather than 2 numbers as in the last example.

EXAMPLE
The length of a piece of string is 100 cm.

The string is now cut into three pieces in the ratio 1 : 4 : 5
Find and write down the length of the shortest piece.

SOLUTION
To find the length of the shortest piece, I first need to find the sum of the numbers in the ratio. I achieve this by adding them together:

$$1 + 4 + 5 = 10$$

I now divide the length of the piece of string which is 100 cm by 10:

$$100 \div 10 = 10$$

To find the length of the three individual pieces I multiply 10 by each number in the ratio i.e. 1, 4 and 5

$$1 \times 10 = 10 \ cm$$

$$4 \times 10 = 40 \ cm$$

$$5 \times 10 = 50 \ cm$$

These are the lengths of the 3 pieces of string. One piece is 10 cm, the other is 40 cm and the final piece is 50 cm. Together they add to make 100 cm, which is the length of the string uncut.

Therefore, the length of the shortest piece of string is 10 cm.

END OF CHAPTER QUESTIONS (RATIOS)

1. There are both chocolate chip cookies and raisin cookies in a jar. The total number of cookies is 56. The ratio of the number of chocolate chip cookies to raisin cookies is 3: 5
   Work out the number of raisin cookies in the jar.

2. There are 12 blue sweets and 6 red sweets in a box. What is the ratio of the number of blue sweets to the number of red sweets? Give your answer in the simplest form.

3. A model of a building is scaled down and has a 3:1 ratio. The real height of the building is 60 metres.
   Calculate the height of the model building in metres.

4. A chocolate bar, 30 cm in length, is split between three friends in the ratio 1: 3: 6.

   a) What is the length of the shortest piece?

   b) What is the length of the longest piece?

5. Write the ratio 26:4 in its simplest form

6. Write the ratio 26:6 in its simplest form

7. Write 36: 14 in its simplest form

CHAPTER 15:
STANDARD FORM

Converting numbers into standard form is useful when dealing with both large and small numbers which contain a lot of zeros. This chapter explains how to convert numbers into standard form.

EXAMPLE
Write 40 000 in standard form

SOLUTION
To tackle this question, these are the steps I take:

$$40\ 000 = 4 \times 10\ 000$$

I can now write 10 000 as 10^4 because:

$$10^4 = 10 \times 10 \times 10 \times 10 = 10\ 000$$

A useful tip is that the number of the power is always the same as the number of zeros. For this example, there are four zeros which is why 10 000 can be written as 10^4.

I now replace 10 000 with 10^4 in the equation:

$$40\ 000 = 4 \times 10^4$$

This is the answer in standard form, 4×10^4

When using a calculator, look for a button that says EXP on it. When this button is pressed, the calculator understands it as $\times 10^{[\ ]}$ and if you now press the number 4 straight after having pressed the EXP button, the calculator sees this as $\times 10^4$.

To calculate 4×10^4 using a calculator, use the following procedure:

Press 4 into a calculator followed by the EXP button followed by the number 4 again and you will get 40 000

EXAMPLE
Write 6×10^3 as an ordinary number

SOLUTION
I know that 10^3 has three zeros, which means:

$$10^3 = 1000$$

Multiplying this by 6 gives:

$$6 \times 10^3 = 6 \times 1000 = 6000$$

EXAMPLE
Write 12000 in standard form

Solution

I can write 12000 as $1.2 \times 10\,000$

Next, I know that $10\,000 = 10^4$ because there are 4 zeros.

So, 12000 in standard form is:

$$12000 = 1.2 \times 10\,000 = 1.2 \times 10^4$$

EXAMPLE
Write 0.0002 into standard form

SOLUTION
$$0.0002 = 2 \times 0.0001$$

Note that there are 3 zeros after the decimal point both before (0.0002) and after (0.0001) the equals sign.

Next, I know that:

$$0.0001 = 10^{-4}$$

Because there are 4 zeros behind the 1, the power becomes negative, compared to the previous examples where the zeros were in front of the 1, making the power positive.

This means that:

$$0.0002 = 2 \times 0.0001 = 2 \times 10^{-4}$$

END OF CHAPTER QUESTIONS (STANDARD FORM)

1. Write the number 240 000 in standard form

2. Write the number 160 000 in standard form

3. Write the number 24 000 in standard form

4. Write the number 16 000 in standard form

5. Write 1.4×10^3 as an ordinary number

6. Write 0.4×10^5 as an ordinary number

7. Write the number 0. 00002 in standard form

8. Calculate $2.4 \times 10^5 - 1.2 \times 10^4$
(Hint: The number to the power of 10 must be the same before a subtraction can take place)

9. Calculate $130 \times 10^4 - 13\ 000 \times 10^2$

10. Write 0.00006 in standard form

CHAPTER 16:
QUADRATIC EQUATIONS

There are a number of methods of solving quadratic equations; however, the quickest and easiest is using the quadratic equation formula once you become familiar with it.

For any quadratic formula in the form $ax^2 + bx + c$ the formula below is valid for calculating the values of x:

$$x = \frac{-b \pm \sqrt{b^2 - 4ac}}{2a}$$

This formula is known as the quadratic equation formula and is always provided in the exam so you do not have to worry about memorising it. It is a useful aid when trying to factorise quadratic formulas in addition to allowing the quadratic equation to be solved. The examples below will demonstrate how this formula works.

EXAMPLE
  a) Solve the following equation

$$x^2 + 5x + 6 = 0$$

  b) Using the values for x calculated in part a), factorise this expression.

SOLUTION

To use the quadratic equation, I must first know what to substitute in for the letters a, b and c which appear in the quadratic formula.

For the expression $x^2 + 5x + 6$:

$a = 1$
$b = 5$
$c = 6$

I can now substitute these values into the quadratic formula:

$$x = \frac{-b \pm \sqrt{b^2 - 4ac}}{2a}$$

$$x = \frac{-5 \pm \sqrt{5^2 - 4 \times 1 \times 6}}{2 \times 1} = \frac{-5 \pm \sqrt{25 - 24}}{2} = \frac{-5 \pm 1}{2}$$

$$x = \frac{-5 - 1}{2} = -\frac{6}{2} = -3 \quad \text{or} \quad x = \frac{-5 + 1}{2} = -\frac{4}{2} = -2$$

Therefore, the solutions to the quadratic equation are: $x = -2$ and -3

To factorise the above expression, simply change the signs in front of both the x's to a sign that is opposite to the one currently there and put them into brackets:

$$(x + 2)\ (x + 3)$$

EXAMPLE

Solve the equation $5x^2 + 12x - 48 = 0$

Give your answer to 2 decimal places.

SOLUTION

The first thing to do is to write down the values of a, b and c so that they are ready to be substituted into the quadratic equation formula:

$a = 5$
$b = 12$
$c = -48$

I now substitute these values into the quadratic equation formula:

$$X = \frac{-b \pm \sqrt{b^2 - 4ac}}{2a} = \frac{-12 \pm \sqrt{12^2 - 4 \times 5 \times (-48)}}{2 \times 5}$$

$$= \frac{-12 \pm \sqrt{144 + 960}}{10} \quad \text{*Remember: two minuses make a plus}$$

$$= \frac{-12 \pm \sqrt{1104}}{10}$$

$x = 2.12$ or $x = -4.52$ (To 2 decimal places, using a calculator)

END OF CHAPTER QUESTIONS (QUADRATIC EQUATIONS)

Solve the following equations, giving your answer to 2 decimal places where necessary:

1. $6x^2 + 10x - 24 = 0$

2. $3x^2 + 12x - 48 = 0$

3. $5x^2 - 25x - 30 = 0$

4. $x^2 + 8x - 48 = 0$

5. $x^2 - 6x + 8 = 0$

6. $x^2 + 8x + 6 = 0$

7. $x^2 - 2x - 8 = 0$

8. a) If $(x - 2)(x - 3) = 12$

   Show that $x^2 - 5x - 6 = 0$

   b) Solve the equation $x^2 - 5x - 6 = 0$

9. a) Factorise the following expression

   $x^2 - 5x - 6 = 0$

b) Solve the equation

$$x^2 - 5x - 6 = 0$$

10. The following is an algebraic fraction:

$$\frac{2}{x-2} - \frac{1}{x-3} = \frac{1}{3}$$

a) Show that it is possible to write this as:

$$x^2 - 8x + 6 = 0$$

b) Use the quadratic equation to solve $x^2 - 8x + 6 = 0$, giving your answer to 2 decimal places.

CHAPTER 17:
FORMULAE AND HOW TO REARRANGE THEM

Formulas are useful for defining a relationship between different things. For example, if someone had the temperature in degrees Celsius (C) and wanted to know what this was in degrees Fahrenheit (F), the following formula would be used:

$$C = \frac{5}{9}\,(F - 32)$$

EXAMPLE
Using the above formula, calculate the temperature in Fahrenheit (F) for a temperature of 20 degrees Celsius (C).

The first thing we will have to do is to rearrange the formula to make F the subject. In every case which has numbers outside of a bracket, we deal with these numbers outside the bracket first so that the bracket has no attachments.

Bringing the 5/9 over the equal sign will make the equation look like:

$$\frac{9}{5}C = (F - 32)$$

Always remember that when a quantity is taken across an equal sign, it becomes *reciprocated* (to be explained shortly) but only if that quantity was multiplied or divided with something else. In this example, the fraction $\frac{5}{9}$ is multiplied by the bracket (F − 32). What this means in simple terms is that the fraction or number or whatever it may be that I want to take over the equal sign (fraction in this case) is put over 1. So, for example, the $\frac{9}{5}$ when taken over the equals sign becomes $\frac{1}{\frac{5}{9}} = \frac{9}{5}$ as seen above.

Now on the right side of the equal sign I have F − 32. To alienate F I must take the −32 which is a negative number on the other side of the equals sign. However, when this needs to be done, the sign on the number I'm moving across the equals sign becomes opposite to what it was before it was transferred across the equals sign. The opposite of a minus sign is a plus sign, so I now have:

$$\frac{9}{5}C + 32 = F$$

I can now plug in the value for C given in the question which is 20 to find F:

$$\frac{9}{5} \times (20) + 32 = F$$

This is fairly easily to calculate without a calculator. Once you have calculated $\frac{9}{5} \times 20 = 36$ all that needs to be done to get the answer simply becomes 36 + 32 = 68 degrees Fahrenheit.

EXAMPLE
Make z the subject of the formula 5 (h + z) = 6 + 8h

Give your answer in its simplest form

SOLUTION
My objective is to isolate z from everything else. Because h is in a bracket, I will need to expand the bracket so that I can use the 8h term on the right hand side to simplify the h in the bracket with.

To do this, I multiply everything in the bracket by 5 giving:

$$5h + 5z = 6 + 8h$$

I can now take the 5h term across the equals sign so that it can be subtracted from the 8h term. The reason why I have decided to take the 5h term across and not the 8h term is because I need to isolate z, so I want the 5z term on its own.

Although you cannot see it, the 5h term has a plus sign in front of it. :

$$+5h + 5z = 6 + 8h$$

Writing the equation like this is the same, but is not normal practice which is why you don't normally see equations with a random + in front of letters or numbers when nothing else precedes it.

The rule is that if there is not a negative sign in front of the letter or number then it is a positive. When I take the 5h term over the equals sign I will need to give it an opposite sign to what's in front of it currently. The opposite of a plus is a minus, so when the 5h term is taken over the equals sign it will be assigned a minus in front of it:

$$5z = 6 + 8h - 5h$$

Simplifying: $8h - 5h = 3h$ which leaves me with:

$$5z = 6 + 3h$$

You may not see a multiplication sign but two quantities joined together mean they are multiplied. I can also write the equation as:

$5 \times z = 6 + 3h$ Which is the same thing as $5z = 6 + 3h$

To completely isolate z I need to divide both sides of the formula by 5. By doing this I will remove the 5 on the left hand side of the equals sign, leaving z on its own while a 5 is used to divide the right hand side of the inequality giving:

$$z = \frac{1}{5}(6 + 3h)$$

This is the neatest and simplest way to give answers for this type of question. Note that I have bracketed the 6 + 3h term. This is because when both sides were divided by 5, all of the right side gets divided, not just a part of it and bracketing the terms in the right hand side is the correct way to ensure that all terms stay together in order to get divided by 5. The equation can also be written as:

$$z = \frac{(6 + 3h)}{5}$$

This shows that everything that was on the right hand side has been divided by 5. Both ways of writing the final answer are equally acceptable as they are essentially the same answer.

END OF CHAPTER QUESTIONS (FORMULAE AND HOW TO REARRANGE THEM)

1. *Expand* $4(3y - 2)$

2. *Expand* $5(y - z)$

3. *Expand* $9(3y + 2)$

4. *Expand* $2x(x + y)$

5. *Expand and simplify* $2(y - 2) + 5(y + 1)$

6. *Simplify* $3x + 2y - 2x + 5y$

7. Make x the subject of the formula $\frac{5y - 1}{x} = 2$

8. Make y the subject of the formula $z = \frac{9}{2}F - y$

9. CDs cost x pounds each and DVDs cost y pounds each. If Sam buys 3 CDs and 2 DVDs, write an expression for the total cost, T.

10. If $x = 2$ and $y = 3$, calculate $z = 12x + 3s$

CHAPTER 18:
INEQUALITIES

This topic follows on from equations. Inequalities are equations, which can be solved, but in place of the equals sign found in normal equations are inequality symbols, such as > (more than), < (less than), ≥ (more than or equal to) and ≤ (less than or equal to).

To understand inequalities, have a look at these number lines:

This number line below represents $x > 2$

This number line shows all numbers greater than 2. The above arrow with stripes at the beginning of it represents x not including the value 2.

This number line below represents $x ≥ 2$

The solid arrow represents x including the value of 2.

The number line below represents $-1 \le x < 3$

$x = 3$ is not included (note the dashed vertical line is slightly offset from 3 to show this) and $x = -1$ is included.

EXAMPLE

x is an integer such that $-1 \le x < 3$. List all the possible values of x.

SOLUTION

An integer means a whole number i.e. a number without a decimal place such as 1, 2, 3 etc. Therefore we need to list all the whole numbers in the interval. Because the interval states $x < 3$ we know that $x = 3$ is not included. Looking at the number line above, we can see that -1, 0, $+1$ *and* $+2$ are all included. Therefore the answer is:

$$-1, 0, +1 \text{ } and \text{ } +2$$

EXAMPLE

Solve the inequality $6x \ge x + 20$

SOLUTION

The only thing that can be done in this situation is to group together the x terms first. The same rules apply for taking a quantity over an inequality sign as they do for taking a quantity over an equals sign. I know that the x to the right of the inequality is positive (remember, if there is not a negative sign in front of the quantity it is a positive). Therefore, when this x is taken over the inequality it will become negative:

$$6x - x \ge 20$$

Simplifying: $5x \ge 20$

To isolate x, divide both sides of the inequality by 5. By doing this it will remove the 5 on the left hand side of the inequality, leaving x on its own while a 5 is used to divide the right hand side of the inequality giving:

$$\frac{5x}{5} \geq 20 \times \frac{1}{5}$$

$\frac{5x}{5} = x$ because the 5's cancel each other and $\frac{20}{5} = 4$ which leads to:

$$x \geq 4$$

EXAMPLE

Find all the solutions for $8 - 4x \geq 24$

SOLUTION

Firstly I must isolate x. To do this I take the 8 across the inequality sign. Remember that it has a positive sign before it (as there isn't a negative minus sign preceding it) which means that when it will be taken across the inequality it becomes negative (in bold below):

$$-4x \geq 24 - 8$$

Once the subtraction is done the equation looks like:

$$-4x \geq 16$$

One rule for solving inequalities is that if you must multiply or divide both sides of the equation by the same negative number, perhaps to isolate a term you are trying to find as above, then the side the inequality is facing changes (for example from $\geq$ to $\leq$).

The next step I must take to isolate x completely is to divide both sides of the equation by negative four (-4), which, according to the rule above means that the side the inequality faces must be changed:

Dividing both sides by -4:

$$-\frac{4x}{-4} \leq \frac{16}{-4}$$

Note that the inequality sign has been turned around. As mentioned in the chapter 'negative numbers', when faced with two minus signs they become positive (shown in bold directly above and below), so the equation now becomes:

$$+\frac{4x}{4} \leq \frac{16}{-4}$$

Simplifying this by carrying out the divisions we get:

$$x \leq -4$$

This means that all numbers which are -4 or less satisfy the inequality.

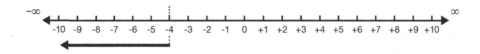

The number line shows the range of numbers which satisfy the inequality. These numbers begin at −4 and go to infinity i.e. never ending.

END OF CHAPTER QUESTIONS (INEQUALITIES)

Solve the following inequalities:

1. $4x + 3 > x + 12$

2. $5x + 2 > 3x + 10$

3. $x + 3 > 2x + 12$

4. $-4x - 3 > x + 12$

5. $6 - 3x > 12$

6. $\dfrac{2x + 3}{2} \leq 3$

7. $\dfrac{3x + 5}{4} \geq 2$

8. $x + 1 \leq 4$

9. $x - 1 \geq -4$

10. $\dfrac{x}{2} + 4 \leq -3$

CHAPTER 19:
SURDS AND SQUARE ROOTS

This chapter aims to give you an introduction to surds.

A surd is a number which is within a square root sign, for example $\sqrt{2}$ is a surd as it cannot be simplified any further. This is the difference between a 'square root' and a surd'.

A number inside a square root can be any number and not just 2. Square roots contain the numbers which can be simplified further, for example $\sqrt{4} = 2$ and therefore $\sqrt{4}$ cannot be classified as a surd but as a square root. This chapter will reveal all the hints and tips needed to tackle both the easy and tough questions involving surds and square roots.

The reason for using surds is that the answers to questions involving surds are accurate and do not need to be rounded off, which means that it is the EXACT answer without even having to make use of a calculator!.

MULTIPLYING SURDS AND SQUARE ROOTS

EXAMPLE
Solve $\sqrt{4} \times \sqrt{4}$

SOLUTION
Firstly, $2 \times 2 = 4$ so taking the square root of 4 will give 2:

$$\sqrt{4} = 2$$

Another way of understanding this is to look at the power or indices of the number. Indices, or powers, are a way of showing how many times a number is multiplied by itself:

2×2 can also be written as 2^2

2^2 is pronounced in everyday English as 'two squared' and the opposite of something squared is the square root of it.

When using powers (indices), a square root is the same thing as $\frac{1}{2}$. This means that I can also write $\sqrt{4}$ as $4^{1/2}$. Both mean the same. If I wanted to take the square root of 2^2 I can either write this as $\sqrt{2 \times 2} = \sqrt{4} = 2$ or I could write it as:

$$(2^{\mathbf{2}})^{\mathbf{1/2}}$$

To calculate this, look at the two indices/powers (numbers in bold). Two powers/indices which appear together as above can be simplified by multiplying them:

$$2 \times \frac{1}{2} = 1$$

Doing this is the shortcut as otherwise I would have needed to expand the whole thing:

$$(2^2)^{1/2} = (2 \times 2)^{1/2} = 2^{1/2} \times 2^{1/2}$$

One of the rules of indices (powers) is that when two numbers containing powers are multiplied, their powers are added together:

$$\frac{1}{2} + \frac{1}{2} = 1$$

This leaves me with $(2^2)^{1/2} = (2 \times 2)^{1/2} = 2^{1/2} \times 2^{1/2} = 2^1$

I now have: 2^1 and anything to the power of 1 remains the same, which means I am left with 2. This shows you that $\sqrt{4}$ (pronounced as 'the square root of four') or, equally the same but written using powers, $4^{1/2}$ (pronounced as 'four to the power of a half') is equal to 2.

Returning to the original question of solving $\sqrt{4} \times \sqrt{4}$, I know that $\sqrt{4} = 2$, so I now must calculate 2 × 2. The answer is 4:

$$\sqrt{4} \times \sqrt{4} = 2 \times 2 = 4$$

EXAMPLE
Calculate $\sqrt{16}$

SOLUTION
The simplest way of solving this question is knowing the 4 times tables and that 4×4=16 which means that $\sqrt{16}$=4.

The answer is 4. But let's examine this question for a little while longer. I want to show you all the manipulations that can be done to this question to get to the same answer. The rules I employ here can be a lifesaver when faced with more complicated questions involving surds and square roots.

With square roots and surds, we can multiply numbers within the square root sign and even create two separate square roots which multiply together as will be shown below:

We can put 4×4 into a square root:

$$\sqrt{16} = \sqrt{4 \times 4}$$

Further to this, we can now separate the 4's inside the square root to make two square roots multiplied together:

$$\sqrt{16} = \sqrt{4 \times 4} = \sqrt{4} \times \sqrt{4}$$

From the previous example, we know that $\sqrt{4}$ = 2 and so this leads us to the final calculation:

$$\sqrt{4} \times \sqrt{4} = 2 \times 2 = 4$$

Note that this answer is exactly the same as the previous example's answer. This is because both examples were exactly the same although you may not have known it as they were displayed differently. The two examples show how we can multiply surds. Remember:

$$\sqrt{xy} = \sqrt{x \times y} = \sqrt{x} \times \sqrt{y}$$

Where x and y are whole numbers (integers).

DIVIDING SURDS AND SQUARE ROOTS

The division of surds are simple. The rule is: $\sqrt{\frac{x}{y}} = \frac{\sqrt{x}}{\sqrt{y}}$ or vice versa. Once this rule is carried out you may find that you will need to use the multiplication rule for surds shown above, so make sure you are familiar with it. The example below demonstrates the importance of knowing the multiplication rule for surds although the question asks for a division of surds.

EXAMPLE
Work out $\sqrt{\frac{25}{64}}$

SOLUTION
Using the division rule:

$$\sqrt{\frac{25}{64}} = \frac{\sqrt{25}}{\sqrt{64}}$$

We now need to calculate $\sqrt{25}$ and $\sqrt{64}$. If you know that $5 \times 5 = 25$ *and* $8 \times 8 = 64$ this will help save time in doing this calculation. If you do find that you have trouble knowing which numbers are likely to be the square root of another number, look at the number in the square root, for example $\sqrt{25}$ above. Then ask yourself which number goes into 25. Let's do this together:

Does 1 go into 25? Yes, but $1 \times 25 = 25$ which is no good as I need two of the **same** numbers multiplied together to give 25.

Does 2 go into 25? No

Does 3 go into 25? No

Does 4 go into 25? No

Does 5 go into 25? **Yes, 5 times** i.e. **5 × 5 = 25**, therefore $\sqrt{25} = 5$

The same thing can be done to find $\sqrt{64}$:

Does 1 go into 64? Yes, but $1 \times 64 = 64$ which is no good as I need two of the **same** numbers multiplied together to give 64.

Does 2 go into 64? Yes, but $2 \times 32 = 64$ which is no good as I need two of the **same** numbers multiplied together to give 64.

Does 3 go into 64? No

Does 4 go into 64? Yes, but 4 × 16 = 64 which is no good as I need two of the **same** numbers multiplied together to give 64.

Does 6 go into 64? No

Does 7 go into 64? No

Does 8 go into 64? **Yes, 8 times** i.e. 8 × 8 = 64, therefore $\sqrt{64} = 8$

As you become more familiar with the times tables, the need for doing this will reduce and eventually, with practice you will begin to memorise certain square roots such as those given in the above examples. Remember the key is to find two of the same numbers which multiply to produce the number contained in the square root.

I have now found that $\sqrt{25} = 5$ and $\sqrt{64} = 8$. The next step becomes:

$$\sqrt{\frac{25}{64}} = \frac{\sqrt{25}}{\sqrt{64}} = \frac{5}{8}$$

Because $\frac{5}{8}$ cannot be reduced any further, this is the final answer.

An alternative method of doing this, knowing that 5 × 5 = 25 and 8 × 8 = 64, is the following:

$$\sqrt{\frac{25}{64}} = \frac{\sqrt{25}}{\sqrt{64}} = \frac{\sqrt{5 \times 5}}{\sqrt{8 \times 8}} = \frac{\sqrt{5} \times \sqrt{5}}{\sqrt{8} \times \sqrt{8}}$$

What I can do now is switch to using powers. Recall that a square root is equivalent to a power of $\frac{1}{2}$ (as shown below).

$$\frac{\sqrt{5} \times \sqrt{5}}{\sqrt{8} \times \sqrt{8}} = \frac{5^{1/2} \times 5^{1/2}}{8^{1/2} \times 8^{1/2}}$$

As mentioned earlier, when two numbers containing powers are multiplied, their powers are added together:

$$a^c \times b^d = ab^{c+d}$$

Even if *a*, *b*, *c* and *d* are all the same numbers, this rule still applies. It is worth memorising this as it will help you with many mathematics questions.

Dealing with the top row (numerator) first:

$$5^{1/2} \times 5^{1/2} = 5^{(1/2 + 1/2)}$$

Adding the two powers (in bold above):

$$\frac{1}{2} + \frac{1}{2} = 1$$

This means I am left with 5^1 and as mentioned earlier; any number raised to the power of 1 remains the same, which means $5^1 = 5$.

Repeating the process for the bottom row (denominator):

$$8^{1/2} \times 8^{1/2} = 8^{(1/2+1/2)}$$

Adding the two powers (in bold above):

$$\frac{1}{2} + \frac{1}{2} = 1$$

This means I am left with 8^1 which means $8^1 = 8$.

Overall:

$$\frac{\sqrt{5} \times \sqrt{5}}{\sqrt{8} \times \sqrt{8}} = \frac{5^{1/2} \times 5^{1/2}}{8^{1/2} \times 8^{1/2}} = \frac{5}{8}$$

This is the same answer I arrived at initially.

SQUARING SURDS

This ties in neatly with what has been discussed in the above examples. Another rule of surds is:

$$(\sqrt{x})^2 = x$$

EXAMPLE
Calculate $(\sqrt{16})^2$

SOLUTION
Do not be tempted to find the square root of 16 as there is no need. Looking at the above rule for surds, $(\sqrt{x})^2 = x$ and our x in this case is 16. So our answer is 16 according to the rule.

However, I will now show you the maths responsible for this rule. Recall that a square root is the equivalent to a power of $\frac{1}{2}$. I can now rewrite the question knowing this fact:

$$(\sqrt{16})^2 = (16^{1/2})^2$$

Recall the short cut discussed above when there are two powers, one inside a bracket and one outside a bracket. We multiply them (two powers in bold above):

$$\frac{1}{2} \times 2 = 1$$

This leaves us with $(\sqrt{16})^2 = (16^{1/2})^2 = 16^1 = 16$ (Remember that any number raised to the power of 1 remains as it is).

The answer to this example is 16.

EXAMPLE
Work out $(2 + \sqrt{5})(2 - \sqrt{5})$

This example put's the rule above to good use as this is a typical exam question.

SOLUTION
The first step to take would be to expand the brackets. For those who are not familiar with expanding brackets, a quick explanation is given below.

Firstly multiply the two numbers on the left of each bracket (circled):

$(②+ \sqrt{5})(②- \sqrt{5})$

$2 \times 2 = 4$

The next step is to multiply the quantity on the right hand side of the left hand bracket with the number on the left of the right hand side bracket (remember to include any positive or negative signs):

$(②+ \sqrt{5})(2 - ⑤)$

$2 \times -\sqrt{5} = -2\sqrt{5}$

The next step is easy to remember, multiply the two quantities that almost meet in the middle from both brackets:

$(2 + \sqrt{5})(2 - \sqrt{5})$

$\sqrt{5} \times 2 = +2\sqrt{5}$ (The plus sign indicates this is a positive quantity as no negatives were involved)

The final step is to multiply the two right hand side quantities on each bracket, once again making a note of the signs:

$(2 + \sqrt{5})(2 - \sqrt{5})$

$\sqrt{5} \times -\sqrt{5} = -(\sqrt{5})^2 = -5$

I now have the following:

$$4 - 2\sqrt{5} + 2\sqrt{5} - 5$$

Simplifying this, the $2\sqrt{5}$ terms cancel each other $-2\sqrt{5} + 2\sqrt{5} = 0$

$4 - 2\sqrt{5} + 2\sqrt{5} - 5$

Leaving me to calculate $4 - 5 = -1$

The answer to this example is **-1**

For questions which have three brackets involved, don't panic, follow the procedure as detailed above for two of those brackets, any two of them, it wouldn't matter which two brackets you choose and this should lead you to the answer.

RATIONALISING SURDS

Rationalising is simply a term used to mean putting any surds found in the denominator (the lower half of a fraction) into the numerator (top half) of a fractional expression. This leads to a neater answer and exam questions could consist of questions which give you a fractional expression with a surd in the denominator and ask you to rationalise it. This section deals with this in detail.

To introduce you to rationalisation, easy examples have been provided which progress onto considerably harder examples. Once you have understood the examples, rationalisation should never be a problem for you again!.

EXAMPLE

Rationalise $\dfrac{3}{\sqrt{3}}$

SOLUTION

To rationalise a fraction containing a surd, multiply the top (numerator) and bottom (denominator) of the fraction by the surd in the denominator of the fraction:

$$\frac{3}{\sqrt{3}} \times \frac{\sqrt{3}}{\sqrt{3}}$$

Multiplying the quantities in the top row of the fraction together:

$$3 \times \sqrt{3} = 3\sqrt{3}$$

Multiplying the two surds in the bottom row together gives:

$$\sqrt{3} \times \sqrt{3} = (\sqrt{3})^2 = 3$$

The final answer looks like:

$$\frac{3}{\sqrt{3}} = \frac{3}{\sqrt{3}} \times \frac{\sqrt{3}}{\sqrt{3}} = \frac{3\sqrt{3}}{3}$$

EXAMPLE

Rationalise $\dfrac{5}{\sqrt{4}}$

SOLUTION

This question can be solved using the same method used in the previous example:

$$\frac{5}{\sqrt{4}} = \frac{5}{\sqrt{4}} \times \frac{\sqrt{4}}{\sqrt{4}} = \frac{5\sqrt{4}}{4}$$

This can be simplified even further, because $\sqrt{4} = 2$ which means:

$$\frac{5\sqrt{4}}{4} = \frac{5 \times 2}{4} = \frac{10}{4}$$

As shown in the fractions chapter, $\dfrac{10}{4}$ can be simplified further because 4 goes into 10 twice with a remainder of 2:

$$\frac{10}{4} = 2\frac{2}{4}$$

This can further be simplified because $\frac{2}{4} = \frac{1}{2}$ which gives:

$$\frac{10}{4} = 2\frac{2}{4} = 2\frac{1}{2}$$

The final answer is therefore $2\frac{1}{2}$

There are other ways of writing this answer, such as multiplying the whole number outside the fraction (2 in this case) with the denominator (also 2 in this case, which leads to the calculation 2 × 2 = 4) and then adding the numerator (1 in this case, making the calculation 4 + 1 = 5). This is then all divided by the current denominator, giving $\frac{5}{2}$:

$$2\frac{1}{2} = \frac{5}{2}$$

Or I can also write the answer as 2.5 in decimal form. They are all the same answer but written in different forms.

The next few examples deal with similar problems, but will involve brackets which make the question slightly harder.

EXAMPLE

Simplify $\frac{3+\sqrt{3}}{2-\sqrt{3}}$

The way to approach these types of questions is to look at the denominator, which is $2 - \sqrt{3}$ in this example. I must firstly multiply the top and bottom halves of the fraction by the denominator. However, note that the denominator contains a negative sign. I must multiply the top and bottom of the fraction by the opposite of this sign i.e. a positive, in order to simplify (the signs referred to here are shown in bold below):

$$\frac{3+\sqrt{3}}{2-\sqrt{3}} = \frac{(3+\sqrt{3})}{(2-\sqrt{3})} \times \frac{(2+\sqrt{3})}{(2+\sqrt{3})} = \frac{(3+\sqrt{3})}{(2-\sqrt{3})}\frac{(2+\sqrt{3})}{(2+\sqrt{3})}$$

Expanding the bracket for the numerator gives me:

$$(3+\sqrt{3})(2+\sqrt{3}) = 6 + 3\sqrt{3} + 2\sqrt{3} + (\sqrt{3})^2 = 6 + 5\sqrt{3} + 3 = \mathbf{9 + 5\sqrt{3}}$$

There are two ways of solving the brackets in the denominator. Either by expanding the brackets using the method shown earlier in the surds chapter (now is a good time to practice expanding brackets if you need to) or by using a useful relationship which is:

$$(a + \sqrt{b})(a - \sqrt{b}) = a^2 - b$$

Both methods are essentially the same; the difference is that using the above relationship would only work if you can remember it. Expanding the brackets yourself would give you the same answer without having to remember any relationship. With practice, it will come naturally and you will be able to see the answer in your mind without even having expanded the brackets believe it or not.

Using the relationship above to expand the brackets in the denominator gives:

$$(2 - \sqrt{3})(2 + \sqrt{3}) = (2)^2 - 3 = 4 - 3 = 1$$

This leaves an overall final answer of:

$$\frac{9 + 5\sqrt{3}}{1} = 9 + 5\sqrt{3}$$

EXAMPLE

Rationalise $\dfrac{4}{7 + 3\sqrt{5}}$

SOLUTION

From the past examples, you should know that for this question you need to multiply both the top and bottom of the fraction by the whole of the denominator quantity and that you will need to use the opposite sign to what is currently in the denominator (that is the sign between the 2 and the $3\sqrt{5}$ which is a plus sign):

$$\frac{4}{7 + 3\sqrt{5}} = \frac{4}{7 + 3\sqrt{5}} \times \frac{(7 - 3\sqrt{5})}{(7 - 3\sqrt{5})}$$

$$= \frac{4}{7 + 3\sqrt{5}} \frac{(7 - 3\sqrt{5})}{(7 - 3\sqrt{5})}$$

The plus and minus signs in bold indicate that the sign needs to be changed when multiplying the top and bottom of the fraction.

Multiplying out the numerator gives: $4(7 - 3\sqrt{5}) = 28 - 12\sqrt{5}$

Multiplying out the denominator using the relationship:

$(a + \sqrt{b})(a - \sqrt{b}) = a^2 - b$

Gives: $(7+3\sqrt{5})7 - 3\sqrt{5} = 7^2 - (3^2 \times 5) = 49 - 45 = 4$

Overall:

$$\frac{28 - 12\sqrt{5}}{4}$$

This can be reduced further:

$$\frac{28 - 12\sqrt{5}}{4} = \frac{28}{4} - \frac{12\sqrt{5}}{4} = \mathbf{7 - 3\sqrt{5}}$$

The final answer is $\mathbf{7 - 3\sqrt{5}}$

REDUCING SURDS

Reducing surds can make the number in the square root smaller. This is useful when simplifying equations, formulas, expressions etc.

EXAMPLE
Reduce $\sqrt{63}$ to its simplest form

SOLUTION
The trick here is to find the highest number which can be squared, which when multiplied by another number makes 63.

How do I find this number initially? Well, try to think of two numbers multiplied together which make 63. The answers to this are, starting from the 1 times table and going upwards:

$1 \times 63 = 63$, this is no good as if I used this I would simply end up repeating the question by putting 63 into a square root sign.

2 does not go into 63

3 × 21 = 63, none of these numbers have a square root so this is no good to me.

4, 5 and 6 do not go into 63 leaving the next number 7, which does:

9 × 7 = 63, this is ideal because 9 can be square rooted to become 3:

$$\sqrt{63} = \sqrt{9 \times 7} = 3\sqrt{7}$$

With all simplify square root questions, remember to follow this logical method and you will find your answer very quickly providing you are good with your times tables.

EXAMPLE
Simplify $\sqrt{24}$

SOLUTION
Starting with the 1 time's table:

1 × 24 = 24, this cannot help me in this case because it leads back to the original question if I square root 24.

2 × 12 = 24, this can work for me but will require the simplification of $\sqrt{12}$, I will get back to this and show you how it's done shortly as I would like to show you the simplest way of solving this question beforehand.

3 × 8 = 24 this can work but will require the simplification of $\sqrt{8}$, I will also get back to this.

4 × 6 = 24, this is the simplest way to solve this question as 4 can be square rooted, i.e. by calculating $\sqrt{4}$ and multiplying this by $\sqrt{6}$ as shown below:

$$\sqrt{24} = \sqrt{4 \times 6}$$
$$= \sqrt{4} \times \sqrt{6}$$
$$= 2\sqrt{6}$$

How to calculate the answer from 2 × 12 = 24:

$$\sqrt{24} = \sqrt{2 \times 12}$$
$$= \sqrt{2} \times \sqrt{12}$$
$$= \sqrt{2} \times \sqrt{4 \times 3}$$

$= \sqrt{2} \times \sqrt{4} \times \sqrt{3}$ (Remember that $\sqrt{4} = 2$)

$= \sqrt{2} \times 2 \times \sqrt{3}$

$= 2\sqrt{2 \times 3}$ (The two separate square roots have been put into one square root)

$= \mathbf{2\sqrt{6}}$

How to calculate the answer from $3 \times 8 = 24$:

$\sqrt{24} = \sqrt{3 \times 8}$

$\qquad = \sqrt{3} \times \sqrt{8}$

$\qquad = \sqrt{3} \times \sqrt{4 \times 2}$

$\qquad = \sqrt{3} \times \sqrt{4} \times \sqrt{2}$ (Remember that $\sqrt{4} = 2$)

$\qquad = \sqrt{3} \times 2 \times \sqrt{2}$

$\qquad = 2\sqrt{2 \times 3}$ (The two separate square roots have been put into one square root)

$\qquad = \mathbf{2\sqrt{6}}$

You should now be able to simplify any number in a square root using the above method. The next example is about as tough as it gets for GCSE maths and you will not be able to find a number that has a square root straight away, but do not be afraid because you are well equipped to deal with it if you have understood the above examples fully.

EXAMPLE
Simplify $\sqrt{1050}$

SOLUTION
When such huge numbers are involved, it is not worth going through the times tables to find a suitable square root. My advice here is to jump straight to a number that would significantly reduce the number in the square root, for example, use the 10 times table as it is easy to work with:

$10 \times 105 = 1050$, you can now see that I have managed to bring down the number in the square root from 1050 to 105, which is much more manageable to work with.

The next step is to put these into square roots:

$$\sqrt{1050} = \sqrt{10 \times 105} = \sqrt{10} \times \sqrt{105}$$

I now need to reduce the 105 further and looking at the number 105 it is easy to see that it is a number divisible by 5:

$= \sqrt{10} \times \sqrt{105}$

$= \sqrt{10} \times \sqrt{5 \times 21}$

Now that there is a 5 in a square root, why don't I create another 5 and pair them up:

$= \sqrt{2 \times 5} \times \sqrt{5 \times 21}$

$= \sqrt{2} \times \sqrt{5} \times \sqrt{5} \times \sqrt{21}$

$= \sqrt{2} \times (\sqrt{5})^2 \times \sqrt{21}$ (Remember the rule $(\sqrt{a})^2 = a$)

$= \sqrt{2} \times 5 \times \sqrt{21}$ (Now I need to combine the two surds into one)

$= \mathbf{5\sqrt{42}}$

This is the final answer; no further simplifications are available to be made. Hopefully these examples have familiarised you with the use of square roots and surds. You are now ready to attempt the end of chapter practice questions.

END OF CHAPTER QUESTIONS (SURDS)

Simplify the following:

1. $(-\sqrt{8})^2$

2. $(-\sqrt{9})^2$

3. $(\sqrt{9})^2$

4. $(\sqrt{8})^2$

5. $(-\sqrt{3})^2$

6. $(\sqrt{3})2$

7. $\sqrt{432}$

8. $\sqrt{288}$

9. $\sqrt{120}$

10. $\sqrt{60}$

Calculate the following by expanding the brackets:

11. $(3 + \sqrt{5})(3 - \sqrt{5})$

12. $(4 + \sqrt{5})(4 - \sqrt{5})$

13. $(5 + \sqrt{5})(5 - \sqrt{5})$

14. $(2 + \sqrt{3})(2 - \sqrt{3})$

15. $(1 + \sqrt{5})(2 - \sqrt{5})$

16. $(9 + \sqrt{2})(2 - \sqrt{2})$

17. $(10 + \sqrt{8})(2 - \sqrt{2})$ *(Hint: $\sqrt{8}=2\sqrt{2}$)

18. $(9 + 4\sqrt{2})(2 - \sqrt{2})$

19. $(2 + 3\sqrt{3})(2 - 2\sqrt{3})$

20. $(5 + 5\sqrt{7})(2 - 4\sqrt{7})$

Rationalise the following. Give your answers in the simplest form possible:

21. $\dfrac{1}{7 + \sqrt{5}}$

22. $\dfrac{1}{3 + \sqrt{5}}$

23. $\dfrac{1}{2 + \sqrt{6}}$

24. $\dfrac{1}{6 + \sqrt{10}}$

25. $\dfrac{1}{7 - \sqrt{5}}$

26. $\dfrac{1}{2 - \sqrt{10}}$

27. $\dfrac{1}{4 + 2\sqrt{7}}$

28. $\dfrac{1}{3 - 2\sqrt{3}}$

29. $\dfrac{2}{4 + \sqrt{5}}$

30. $\dfrac{7}{11 - 2\sqrt{10}}$

31. $\dfrac{3}{2 + 3\sqrt{3}}$

Simplify the following, giving your answer in the simplest form possible:

32. $\dfrac{2 + \sqrt{3}}{2 - \sqrt{3}}$

33. $\dfrac{3 + \sqrt{3}}{7 + \sqrt{3}}$

34. $\dfrac{5 + 3\sqrt{3}}{2 - 2\sqrt{3}}$

35. $\dfrac{3 - 7\sqrt{3}}{8 + \sqrt{3}}$

36. $\dfrac{10 + 3\sqrt{8}}{7 - \sqrt{8}}$

37. $\dfrac{4 - 2\sqrt{3}}{5 - 6\sqrt{3}}$

CHAPTER 20:
POWERS AND INDICES

You may be wondering what the difference in meaning is between the word 'power' and 'indices'. Put simply, a power (also known as an index) is used to write the product of numbers in a way that uses the least space possible on a page e.g. rather than writing 3 × 3, using powers this would be 3^2 (read as 3 raised to the power of 2 or three squared). When I refer to two or more powers, these are known as **indices**.

A quick explanation of how powers work is shown below:

$$3^2 = 3 \times 3$$

$$2^2 = 2 \times 2$$

$$3^3 = 3 \times 3 \times 3$$

$$a^5 = a \times a \times a \times a \times a$$

Hopefully you can see that using powers is a short cut. Rather than having to multiply out every number, the entire sum can conveniently be written in a power/index format.

During this chapter, I will be using terminology you may not be familiar with yet, so I will briefly explain using x^y as an example:

For x^y, the power/index is y and the base number is x.

There are a number of rules which need to be learnt when working with indices. The following need to be memorised:

Rule 1: $\quad x^y \times x^z = x^{y+z}$

Rule 1 demonstrates that two expressions consisting of the same base have their powers added together. For example, $2^2 \times 2^1 = 2^{2+1} = 2^3$

Rule 2: $\quad x^0 = 1$ and $x^1 = x$

Rule 2 demonstrates that any expression raised to the power of zero is equal to 1 and any expression raised to the power of 1 is equal to the base which is being raised to the power of 1. For example, $2^0 = 1$ *and* $2^1 = 2$

Rule 3: $\quad \dfrac{x^y}{x^z} = x^{y-z}$

Rule 3 demonstrates that when two expressions consisting of the same base are divided their indices are subtracted. For example,

$$\frac{2^2}{2^1} = 2^{2-1} = 2^1$$

Rule 4: $\quad (x^y)^z = x^{y \times z} = x^{yz}$

Rule 4 demonstrates that two powers which are directly next to each other are multiplied. For example, $(5^2)^3 = 5^{2 \times 3} = 5^6$

Rule 5: $\quad x^{-y} = \dfrac{1}{x^y}$

Rule 5 demonstrates that a negative power causes the base expression to be divided by 1. For example,

$$3^{-1} = \frac{1}{3^1}$$

Rule 6: $\quad x^{1/y} = \sqrt[y]{x}$

Rule 6 demonstrates that when a base is raised to the power of a fractional expression, the base becomes square rooted by the denominator of that fractional expression. Examples are:

$4^{1/2} = \sqrt[2]{4}$. This is read as 'the square root of 4'.

The answer is 2 because $2 \times 2 = 4$

$27^{1/3} = \sqrt[3]{27} = 3$. This is read as 'the cube root of 27'.

The answer is 3 because $3 \times 3 \times 3 = 27$

$\sqrt[4]{16} = 2$

The answer is 2 because if I multiplied 2 four times, I get 16, which is the number inside the root sign: $2 \times 2 \times 2 \times 2 = 16$

Rule 7: $\quad x^{z/y} = (\sqrt[y]{x})^z$

Rule 7 is an extension of rule 6 and shows what the numerator of the fractional power does to the initial expression.

Now that the basic rules have been covered, I will go through some examples to put these rules into action.

EXAMPLE

Using the appropriate rules, simplify the following:

  i) $7^0 \times 7^1$
  ii) $(7^1)^{1/3}$
  iii) $12^{1/3} \times 12^{-1/3}$
  iv) $16^5 \div 16^1$

SOLUTION
  i) $7^0 \times 7^1 = 7^{0+1} = 7^1$ *(USING RULE 1)*
  ii) $(7^1)^{1/3} = 7^{1 \times 1/3} = 7^{1/3}$ *(USING RULE 4)*
  iii) $12^{1/3} \times 12^{-1/3} = 12^{(1/3+1/3)} = 12^{2/3}$ *(USING RULE 1)*
  iv) $16^5 \div 16^1 = 16^{5-1} = 16^4$ *(USING RULE 3)*

EXAMPLE

Calculate the following:

    i) $27^{1/3} \times 27^{1/3}$

    ii) $(8^2)^{1/3}$

    iii) $12^{1/3} \times 12^{-1/3}$

    iv) $16^5 \div 16^5$

    v) $\dfrac{16^3}{16^3}$

SOLUTIONS

    i) $27^{1/3} \times 27^{1/3} = 27^{(1/3+1/3)} = 27^{2/3} = (\sqrt[3]{27})^2 = 3^2 = 9$ *(USING RULES 1 AND 7)*

    ii) $(8^2)^{1/3} = 8^{2 \times 1/3} = 8^{2/3} = (\sqrt[3]{8})^2 = (2)^2 = 2 \times 2 = 4$ *(USING RULES 4 AND 7)*

    iii) $12^{1/3} \times 12^{-1/3} = 12^{1/3+(-1/3)} = 12^{1/3-1/3} = 12^0 = 1$ *(USING RULE 1)*

    iv) $16^5 \div 16^5 = 16^{5-5} = 16^0 = 1$ *(USING RULE 3)*

    v) $\dfrac{16^3}{16^3} = 16^{3-3} = 16^0 = 1$ *(USING RULE 3)*

These are the basic rules of indices. Everything with regard to indices revolves around these rules so make sure you learn them.

END OF CHAPTER QUESTIONS (INDICES)

Calculate the following:

    1. 2^0

    2. 4^0

    3. 8^0

    4. 200^0

    5. 555^0

    6. 4^{-2}

7. 3^{-2}

8. 5^{-2}

9. 2^{-3}

10. 4^2

11. 2^2

12. $4^2 \times 4^{-2}$

13. $\dfrac{4^{-2}}{4^{-3}}$

14. $(2^2)^2$

Simplify the following:

15. $x^2 \times x^4$

16. $b^3 \times b^5$

17. $y(xy^2 \times yx^4)$

18. $(x^2)^3$

19. $\dfrac{x^2y^2}{xy}$

20. $(x^5yz^2)^3$

21. $\dfrac{x^2yz^3 + x^5y^2z^2}{xyz}$

22. $\dfrac{p^5q^2r^3(ab) + p^3q^3r^7(a^3b)}{pq^2r^2b}$

23. $(z^{1/3})^3$

24. $(x^{-1/2})^{-1/2}$

25. $\dfrac{xy^3}{x^{1/2}y^2}$

CHAPTER 21:
FACTORISATION

In your exam, you may be asked to factorise an expression or simplify algebraic expressions which will require you to use factorisation in order to be able to successfully simplify. This chapter aims to get you comfortable with factorisation and simplification techniques.

EXAMPLE
Factorise $x^2 - 10x + 24$

SOLUTION
The very first thing I do with factorisation questions such as the one in this example is to find the number which is not multiplied with x. In this example, the only number not associated with a x term is the number 24. I also need to look at the number which is associated with an x term and in this example, it is the number 10 from $10x$.

Now that I have found these numbers, I need to think of two numbers which make 24 when multiplied together and I also need to make sure that these two numbers, when added together, make 10. This is my initial criteria. I will start with the 1 times table and work my way up to find suitable numbers:

$$1 \times 24 = 24$$
$$1 + 24 = 25$$
$$2 \times 12 = 24$$
$$2 + 12 = 14$$
$$3 \times 8 = 24$$
$$3 + 8 = 11$$

None of these are suitable as they do not total 10 when added together.

$4{\times}6{=}24$
$4{+}6{=}10$ }

This matches my initial criteria of needing two numbers which multiply together to make 24 and add to make a sum of 10.

It is now possible to create brackets with these two numbers:

$$(x - 4)(x - 6)$$

Note that I have put a negative sign in front of both numbers in the brackets. This is because in the question:

$$x^2 - 10x + 24$$

The 24 is positive and the $-10x$ is a negative term. The only way I could achieve making the 24 positive and the 10 negative is to have both numbers negative. Let's go through expanding this bracket so that you can see exactly what I mean. Expanding the brackets is also a useful check to see if I have factorised correctly. If I have, the expansion of the brackets should lead to the original question.

To expand $(x - 4)(x - 6)$:

- I start by multiplying the two x's from both brackets to give the x^2 term, $x \times x = x^2$

- Next I multiply the x from the left bracket with the -6 in the bracket on the right to give $x \times - 6 = -6x$.

- Next I multiply the -4 in the left bracket with the x in the right bracket to give $-4 \times x = -4x$

- Finally, I multiply the -4 in the left bracket with the 6 in the bracket on the right to give $-4 \times 6 = -24$

Summing all the terms above, I have:

$$x^2 - 6x - 4x + 24$$

Finally, $- 6x - 4x = -10x$ (Don't let the negative signs confuse you. The best way to deal with this is to simply treat the 6 and 4 as being positive as if you are calculating a normal addition, but stick a negative in front of the answer).

This leads me to the original question:

$$x^2 - 10x + 24$$

Hopefully this has shown you the importance of getting the signs right. A very useful check when asked to factorise expressions is that once the factorisation is done, expand the brackets straight away as I have done above and if you find that you arrive at the original question, you have factorised correctly. If not, then you should go through your working out again step by step to see exactly where you may have gone wrong.

EXAMPLE
Factorise completely $3x^9 - 300x$

SOLUTION
The first thing I notice is a 3 and a 300. This means I can leave 3 outside a bracket and also, because both terms in the above equation have x's in them, I can also take out one x and leave it outside any brackets. Note that I am only able to remove the x with the lowest power. In this example, this would be x^1 which appears as just x in the above equation. This gives:

$$3x(x^8 - 100)$$

Can you see that if you were to multiply out the bracket you would get the original equation?. If not, below are the exact steps to multiply out this bracket:

Step 1: $3x \times x^8 = 3x^{1+8} = 3x^9$ (Remember from the indices chapter that indices are added when two similar bases are multiplied)

Step 2: $3x \times -100 = -300x$ (This was a simple multiplication involving a negative)

Now add step 2 and 3: $3x^9 - 300x$ (This is the equation given in the example)

The above is proof that I can put the initial equation in the form:

$$3x(x^8 - 100)$$

Continuing, I now factorise further:

$$3x(x^4 - 10)(x^4 + 10)$$

Note that one bracket had to be positive and the other negative in order to maintain the -100 found in the equation: $3x(x^8 - 100)$

Therefore, $3x9 - 300x$ in a completely factorised form is:

$$3x(x^4 - 10)(x^4 + 10)$$

END OF CHAPTER QUESTIONS (FACTORISATION)

Factorise the following:

1. $x^2 + 7x + 12$

2. $x^2 - x - 2$

3. $x^2 + 5x + 6$

4. $x^2 - 8x + 15$

5. $x^2 - 4x + 3$

6. $9x^2 + 12x + 4$

7. $x^2 - y^2$

8. $x^2 - 2x - 8$

9. $12x - 3x^2$

10. $x^2 + 8x + 12$

11. $x^2 - 25$

12. $4x^2 - 9$

CHAPTER 22:
SEQUENCES

A sequence is the term used to describe a series of numbers which are related through a common relationship. Commonly, for your GCSE maths exam, you will be asked to find the next number in a sequence or to calculate the nth term of a sequence. You could also be given an nth term and asked to find terms in a sequence. This chapter will reveal all you need to know to succeed in this topic.

FINDING THE NTH TERM

If in the exam you are faced with a sequence which has a common difference between the numbers and you are asked to calculate the nth term, the formula to use for finding the nth term is:

$$dn + (f - d)$$

Where,

d = Difference between every number in the sequence

f = The first number in the sequence

EXAMPLE
Find the nth term of the following sequence:

3, 6, 9, 12, 15 ...

SOLUTION

The first number in the sequence is 3, which means that $f = 3$

The difference between every number in the sequence is 3. Therefore, $d = 3$

Using the formula:

$$dn + (f - d)$$

The nth term is:

$$3n + (3 - 3) = 3n$$

I can also test if this really is the nth term for this sequence by selecting a number for n. For example, if I want to know what the third number is in the above sequence I need to set $n = 3$, which gives:

$$3n = 3 \times 3$$

$$= 9$$

This is correct. The third number in the sequence is indeed 9.

If you are faced with a sequence where the difference between every number in the sequence is not a constant and you are asked to calculate the nth term, the formula to use is:

$$f + (n - 1) d_1 + \frac{(n - 1)(n - 2)}{2} d_2$$

Where,

$f = $ The first number in the sequence

d_1 The difference between the very first two numbers in the sequence

d_2 The number the difference is increasing by.

EXAMPLE

Find the nth term for the following sequence:

2, 5, 9, 14, 20, ...

SOLUTION

The difference between 5 and 2 is $5 - 2 = $ **3** (this is d_1)

The difference between 9 and 5 is $9 - 5 = $ **4**

The difference between 14 and 9 is 14 − 9 = **5**

The difference between 20 and 14 is 20 − 14 = **6**

The numbers in bold above are the first set of differences:

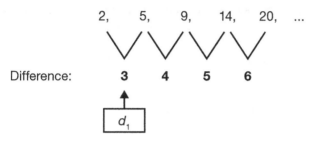

I now need to find the differences between the numbers in bold:

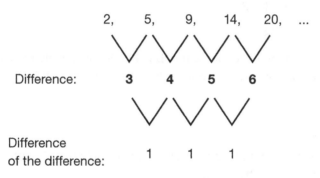

The difference is increasing by 1 each time. Therefore, $d_2 = 1$

The only thing I now need to calculate the nth term is the first number in the sequence, f and $f = 3$.

Using the formula:

$$f + (n - 1)\, d_1 + \frac{(n - 1)(n - 2)}{2}\, d_2$$

And inputting the correct numbers to calculate the nth term I get:

$$2 + (n - 1)\, 3 + \frac{(n - 1)(n - 2)}{2}\, 1$$

Tidying this up, I get:

$$2 + (n - 1)\, 3 + \frac{1}{2}(n - 1)(n - 2)$$

I will give this formula a quick check to see that it works. I want to know what the fourth number in the sequence is. So I set $n = 4$:

$$2 + 3(4 - 1) + \frac{1}{2}(4 - 1)(4 - 2)$$

$$= 2 + 3(3) + \frac{1}{2}(3)(2)$$

$$= 2 + 9 + \frac{1}{2}(6)$$

$$= 11 + 3$$

$$= \mathbf{14}$$

Is the fourth number in the sequence a number 14? Yes, it is, which means that I have correctly calculated a formula to find the nth term for this particular sequence.

EXAMPLE

The nth term of a number sequence is given by the formula $n^2 - 2$. Write down the first four terms of the sequence.

SOLUTION

The 1st term can be found by substituting $n = 1$ into the formula $n^2 - 1$:

$$(1)^2 - 1 = 1 - 1$$

$$= 0$$

The 2nd term can be found by substituting $n = 2$ into the formula $n^2 - 1$:

$$(2)^2 - 1 = 4 - 1$$

$$= 3$$

The 3rd term can be found by substituting $n = 3$ into the formula $n^2 - 1$:

$$(3)^2 - 1 = 9 - 1$$

$$= 8$$

The 4th term can be found by substituting $n = 4$ into the formula $n^2 - 1$:

$$(4)^2 - 1 = 15$$

Therefore, the first four terms of the sequence are:

$$0, 3, 8, 15$$

END OF CHAPTER PRACTICE QUESTIONS (NTH TERMS)

1. The nth term of a number sequence is given by the formula $n^3 - 1$
   Write down the first four terms of the sequence.

2. Here are the first 5 terms of a number sequence.

   25   23   21   19.   17   ...

   a) Write down the next term in the number sequence

   b) Write down the tenth term of this sequence

   c) The number 6 cannot be a term in this number sequence.
      Explain why.

3. Here are the first 6 numbers from a number sequence.

   6   12   18   24   30   36   ...

   Write down an expression, in terms of n, for the nth term of the
   sequence.

4. Calculate the nth term for the following sequence of numbers.

   3   5   9   15   23   ...

CHAPTER 23:
SIMULTANEOUS EQUATIONS

Simultaneous equations are two or more equations which contain two or more unknowns, such as x and y. There are three ways to solve simultaneous equations. I will only be covering one of these as I believe it is the quickest and most efficient way to solve simultaneous equations. The ways of solving simultaneous equations are:

- Elimination method: By far the quickest and easiest way of solving simultaneous equations (shown below)

- Substitution method: Long winded and could get messy when dealing with large numbers.

- Plotting the two equations on a graph: The point where the two graphs intersect is the solution. This will take time and in an exam it would be time you cannot afford to lose.

EXAMPLE
Solve the following pair of simultaneous equations.

$$2x + 6y = 28$$

$$5x + 6y = 2$$

SOLUTION USING THE 'ELIMINATION' METHOD
This involves subtracting the two equations so that I end up with one equation with only one unknown which can be solved. I will firstly label the equations (1) and (2):

$$2x + 6y = 28 \qquad (1)$$

$$5x + 6y = 2 \qquad (2)$$

Subtracting equation (1) from (2) gives:

(1) – (2): $-3x = 24$

$$x = \frac{24}{-3}$$

$$x = -8$$

Now that I know $x = -8$, I can choose to substitute this back into equation (1) or (2) to find the value of y. Substituting $x = 8$ into equation (1) gives:

$2(-8) + 6y = 26$

$-16 + 6y = 26$

$6y = 26 + 16$

$6y = 42$

$y = 7$

The answer to the question is

$$x = -8 \text{ and } y = 7$$

EXAMPLE
Solve the following pair of simultaneous equations:

$$6x + 2y = 6 \qquad (1)$$

$$4x + y = 12 \qquad (2)$$

SOLUTION USING THE 'ELIMINATION' METHOD
This example is slightly harder than the previous example. This is because if I subtracted equation (1) from (2) I would still remain with two unknowns which means there is no way for me to solve the equation.

The way around this is to multiply equation (2) by 2 and label it equation (3). By doing this, I will make the y term a $2y$ which will allow me to subtract the two equations and eliminate the *y* variable:

Equation (2) × 2: $\qquad$ $8x + 2y = 24$ $\qquad$ (3)

I can now eliminate the variable *y* by subtracting equation (3) from equation (1). The reason I have decided to subtract equation (3) from (1) and not the other way around is because doing it this way I avoid dealing with negative numbers:

Equation 3 – Equation (1): $\quad$

$$8x + 2y = 24$$
$$-\ 6x + 2y = 6$$
$$\overline{}$$
$$2x \qquad = 18$$
$$x = \frac{18}{2}$$
$$x = 9$$

Now that I know $x = 9$ I can substitute this back into either equation (1), (2) or (3), I will choose (1) for no particular reason other than I had to choose one equation to substitute $x = 9$ into:

Substituting $x = 9$ into equation (1):

$$6 \times (9) + 2y = 6$$
$$54 + 2y = 6$$
$$2y = -48$$
$$y = -\frac{48}{2}$$
$$y = -24$$

Therefore, the answer to this example is: **$x = 9$ and $y = -24$**

EXAMPLE
Solve the following pair of simultaneous equations

$$4x - 3y = 5$$
$$-4x + 8y = 0$$

SOLUTION USING THE 'ELIMINATION' METHOD

The first action I take is to label both equations (1) and (2):

$$4x - 3y = 5 \quad (1)$$

$$-4x + 8y = 0 \quad (2)$$

Because there are two similar terms in both equations, the $4x$ term, there will be no need to multiply any of the equations by another number as I can eliminate the x term. However, unlike previous examples, I now *add* the two equations rather than subtract them. This is because equation (2) has a negative $4x$ term and I need to keep it negative so that it gets eliminated. I can keep the $-4x$ term negative by adding as, from the directed numbers chapter, a positive and a negative makes a negative (see below):

$$4x + (-4x) = 4x - 4x = 0$$

Adding equation (1) to equation (2):

$$4x - 3y = 5$$
$$+$$
$$-4x + 8y = 0$$
$$\overline{}$$
$$5y = 5$$

$$y = \frac{5}{5}$$

$$y = 1$$

Now that I know $y = 1$ I can substitute this into either equation (1) or (2):

Substituting $y = 1$ into equation (1) gives: $4x - 3(1) = 5$

$$4x - 3 = 5$$

$$4x = 8$$

$$x = 2$$

The answer to this example is **$x = 2$ and $y = 1$**

EXAMPLE

Solve the following pair of simultaneous equations:

$$-4x - 3y = 5$$

$$-4x + 7y = 0$$

SOLUTION USING THE 'ELIMINATION' METHOD:
I firstly label the equations:

$$-4x - 3y = 5 \qquad (1)$$

$$-4x + 7y = 0 \qquad (2)$$

This is a similar question to the previous one. The only difference is that equation (1) now also has a negative $4x$ term. I now think about how I can eliminate the variable x. If I subtract equation (1) from equation (2), the $-4x$ on equation (1) becomes a positive as shown below because two negatives give a positive result:

$$-4x - (-4x) = -4x + 4x = 0$$

This means that I must subtract equation (1) from equation (2):

$$4x - 3y = 20$$
$$- \quad -4x + 7y = 10$$
$$\overline{-10y = 10}$$
$$y = -1$$

Substituting this back into equation (2) gives:

$$-4x + 8(-1) = 0$$

$$-4x - (8) = 0$$

$$-4x = 8$$

$$x = -2$$

The answer to this example is **$x = -2$ and $y = -1$**

EXAMPLE
Solve the following pair of simultaneous equations:

$$-5x - 6y = 9$$

$$-4x - 8y = 0$$

SOLUTION USING THE 'ELIMINATION' METHOD:
The first step is to label the two equations as (1) and (2):

$$-5x - 6y = 9 \quad (1)$$
$$-4x - 8y = 0 \quad (2)$$

The next step is to find the lowest common multiple of either the numbers in front of the x terms (5 and 4) on either equations or the numbers in front of the y terms (6 and 8):

To refresh your memory from the lowest common multiple chapter, the LCM is the lowest number which will divide exactly into all the numbers for which we are trying to find a lowest common multiple, in this case (5 and 4) or (6 and 8). This can be achieved by adding the largest number each time to get the LCM:

To find the lowest common multiple of 5 and 4 multiply the largest number starting with the 1 times table and work upwards:

$5 \times 1 = 5$ (This is not the LCM as 4 does not go into 5)

$5 \times 2 = 10$ (This is not the LCM as 4 does not go into 10)

$5 \times 3 = 15$ (This is not the LCM as 4 does not go into 15)

$5 \times 4 = 20$ (This IS the LCM as both 5 and 4 go into 20)

The same method is used to find the lowest common multiple of 6 and 8. I start with 8×1:

$8 \times 1 = 8$ (This is not the LCM as 6 does not go into 8)

$8 \times 2 = 16$ (This is not the LCM as 6 does not go into 16)

$8 \times 3 = 24$ (This IS the LCM as both 6 and 8 go into 24)

Because the numbers 5 and 4 are associated with the x term and have the lowest number as their lowest common multiple when compared to the 6 and 8 from the x terms, which have an LCM of 24, I will now multiply both equations accordingly so that the x term can be eliminated. To do this I need to multiply both equations so that the x term in both equations becomes $20x$ i.e. the LCM. This is achieved by multiplying equation (1) by 4 and equation (2) by 5:

Equation (1) $\times 4 = -20x - 24y = 32$

Equation (2) $\times 5 = -20x - 40y = 0$

I must now label these two new equations (3) and (4):

$$-20x - 24y = 32 \qquad (3)$$
$$-20x - 40y = 0 \qquad (4)$$

It is now easy to eliminate x:

Remember that two negative's make a positive:

$$-20x - (-20x) = -20x + 20x = 0 \quad \text{and} \quad -24y - (-40y) = -24y + 40y = 16y$$

Equation (3) – Equation (4):

$$\begin{array}{r} -20x - 24y = 32 \quad (3) \\ -\ \underline{-20x - 40y = 0 \quad (4)} \\ 16y = 32 \\ y = 2 \end{array}$$

Now that I know $y = 2$, I can substitute this back into equation (1), (2), (3) or (4). I will choose (1) for no particular reason other than I had to choose one of the 4 equations:

Substituting $y = 2$ into equation (1):

$$-5x - 6y = 8 \qquad (1)$$
$$-5x - 6(2) = 8$$
$$-5x - 12 = 8$$
$$-5x = 8 + 12$$
$$-5x = 20$$
$$x = -4$$

The answer to this example is **x = –4, y = 2**

HOW TO CHECK YOUR ANSWERS

To check your answers, simply substitute your answers back into any of the equations and you should get the answer after the equals sign (in bold below). For example, taking the answers from the example above and inserting them into equation (1), it becomes apparent that the answers are correct:

x = –4, y = 2

$$-5x - 6y = 8 \qquad (1)$$

$$-5(-4) - 6(2) = 20 - 12 = 8$$

You could be asked in the exam to solve a simultaneous equation using a graph that has been provided. To solve the simultaneous equation, always find the point of intersection. The coordinates of the point of intersection are the solution to the simultaneous equation, see the example below.

EXAMPLE

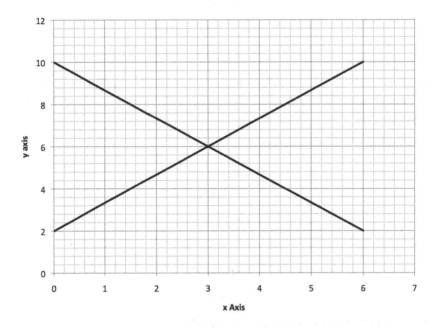

The diagram above shows the graphs of

$$y = \frac{4}{3}x + 2 \qquad \text{and} \qquad 3y + 4x = 10$$

Use the diagram to solve the simultaneous equations

$$y = \frac{4}{3}x + 2$$

$$3y + 4x = 10$$

SOLUTION

The solution is given by the coordinates (x,y) of the point of intersection. Both graphs 'meet' at the point $x = 3$ and $y = 6$ coordinates (3, 6) which means the solution to the simultaneous equations is:

$$x = 3 \text{ and } y = 6$$

END OF CHAPTER QUESTIONS (SIMULTANEOUS EQUATIONS)

1. Solve the following pair of simultaneous equations

$$3x + 2y = 1$$
$$2x - y = 10$$

2. Solve the following pair of simultaneous equations

$$3x + 2y = 7$$
$$2x - 5y = 8$$

3. Solve the following pair of simultaneous equations

$$8x - 3y = 16$$
$$2x - y = 4$$

4. Solve the following pair of simultaneous equations

$$3x + 2y = 23$$
$$-2x + 5y = 29$$

5. Solve the following pair of simultaneous equations

$$3x + 4y = 11$$
$$6x - 5y = -4$$

6. Solve the following pair of simultaneous equations

$$7x + 3y = 1$$
$$x + 2y = -3$$

7. Solve the following pair of simultaneous equations

$$x + y = 1$$
$$4x + 3y = -1$$

CHAPTER 24:
GRAPHS

EXAMPLE

On the grid below, draw the graph of $y = (2 + x)(2 - x)$ for values of x from -2 to +4

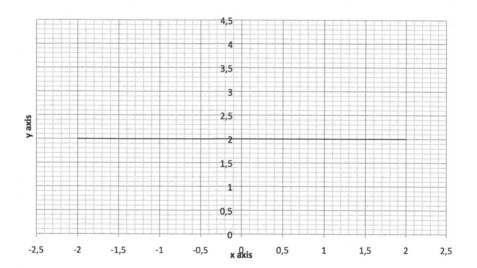

SOLUTION

This is simply a case of plotting a graph. I find it easier to make a quick table listing all the values of y when x varies between –2 to +4 by substituting the values of x into the formula $y = (2 + x)(2 - x)$.

In the exam you may find a partially completed table which you will be asked to complete.

Value of x	Value of y $y = (2 + x)(2 - x)$
-2	$y = (2 + (-2))(2 - (-2))$ $= (2 - 2)(2 + 2)$ $= 0 \times 4$ $= 0$
-1	$y = (2 + (-1))(2 - (-1))$ $= (2 - 1)(2 + 1)$ $= 1 \times 3$ $= 3$
0	$y = (2 + 0)(2 - 0)$ $= 2 \times 2$ $= 4$
1	$y = (2 + 1)(2 - 1)$ $= 3 \times 1$ $= 3$
2	$y = (2 + 2)(2 - 2)$ $= 4 \times 0$ $= 0$
3	$y = (2 + 3)(2 - 3)$ $= 5 \times (-1)$ $= -5$
4	$y = (2 + 4)(2 - 4)$ $= 6 \times (-2)$ $= -12$

I can now plot the graph:

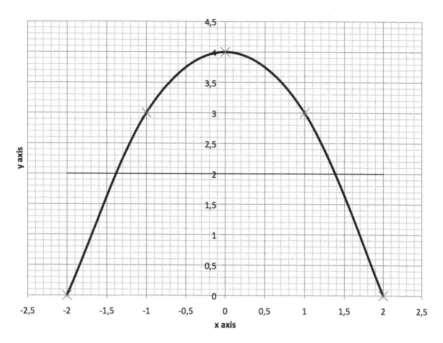

EQUATIONS OF A STRAIGHT LINE

There are a few terms which you need to be familiar with when it comes to straight line graph equations and these are:

'Parallel', 'y-intercept' and 'gradient'.

These terms will be explained throughout this chapter through the use of examples, however, a quick explanation to each term is provided below:

The y-intercept is the point where the straight line hits the y axis of the graph. The gradient is the mathematical term given to the steepness of the straight line plotted on a graph. It can easily be calculated (see examples below).

If two lines are parallel, it means they have the same steepness i.e. same gradient.

EXAMPLE

Write down the equation of the straight line that passes through the point (0, 1) and is parallel to the line $y = \frac{1}{2}x + 2$

SOLUTION

The equation for all straight lines is $y = mx + c$ where m is the gradient and c is the y-intercept.

Because the equation of the straight line I am trying to find is parallel to $y = \frac{1}{2}x + 2$, I know that they both share the same gradient which is $\frac{1}{2}$

Therefore, I already know that the equation of the straight line I am trying to find will have $m = \frac{1}{2}$

$$y = \frac{1}{2}x + c$$

I also know that the line whose equation I am trying to establish passes through the point (0, 1). This is useful as I need to find c, the y-intercept. Substituting in the point (0, 1) will give me the value of c:

$$1 = \frac{1}{2}0 + c$$

$$1 = c$$

I have now found that $c = 1$, which means that I can write the full equation of the straight line, which is:

$$y = \frac{1}{2}x + 1$$

END OF CHAPTER QUESTIONS (STRAIGHT LINE GRAPHS)

1. Write down the equation of the straight line that passes through the point (0, 5) and is parallel to the line $y = \frac{1}{2}x + 2$

2. Write down the equation of the straight line that passes through the point (2, 3) and is parallel to the line $y = \frac{5}{6}x + 1$

3. Write down the equation of the straight line that passes through the point (3, 5) and is parallel to the line $3y = 2x + 3$

4. a) For the equation $y = 2x + 1$, complete the table below:

x	-2	-1	0	1	2
y			1	3	5

b) On the grid below, draw the graph of $y = 2x + 1$, including all the points in the table from part a)

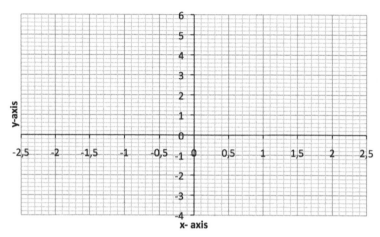

5. In the diagram below, the straight lines passes through the points A (0, −2) and B (6, 2). The point C is (0, 2).

Find the equation of the straight line that passes point C and is parallel to AB.

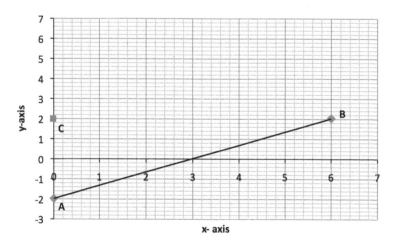

CHAPTER 25: TRANSFORMING GRAPHS

When transforming graphs, it is common to use the notation $f(x)$. When dealing with the topic of graph transformations, $f(x)$ replaces y and stands for a function of x, which in everyday English means 'doing something to x to get the answer required e.g. multiplying x with a quantity, adding a quantity to x etc'.

A quick example of $f(x)$ in action would be:

$$f(x) = 2x + 1$$

When $x = 1$,

$$f(1)=2 \times (1) + 1 = 3$$

When $x = 2$,

$$f(2)=2 \times (2) + 1 = 5$$

This notation is used in exam questions.

The basic rules, using the equation $f(x) = x^2$ and $a = 2$, of transforming graphs are as follows:

$f(x) + a$ Moves the graph up by a units

$f(x) - a$ Moves the graph down by a units

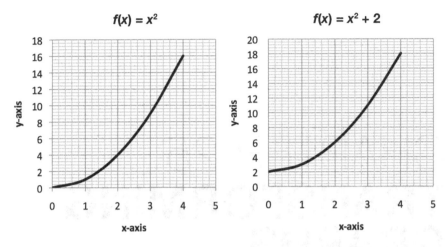

af(x)   Multiplies every *y* value on the graph by the value of *a*.

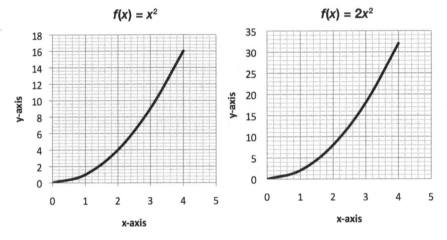

f(x + a)   Shifts the entire graph to the left by *a* units.

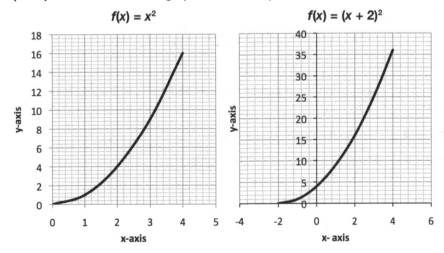

f(x – a) Shifts the entire graph to the right by *a* units

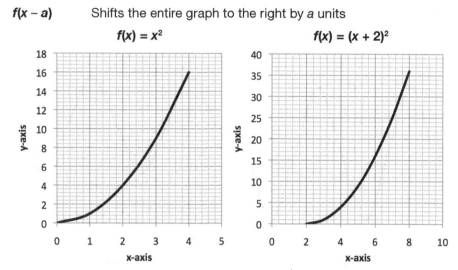

f(ax) Stretches the *x* axis by a scale factor of $\frac{1}{a}$.

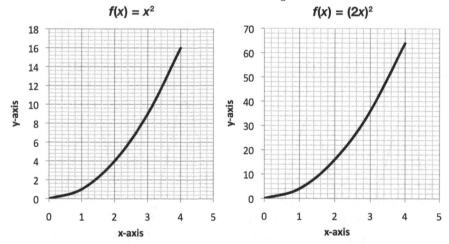

The above transformations may appear clearer on a f(x) = sin(x) graph. Once again, using a = 2:

f(x) + a   Moves the graph up by *a* units

f(x) = sin(x)

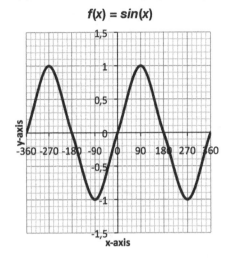

f(x) = sin(x) + 2

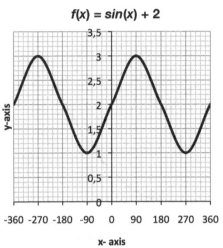

af(x)   Multiplies *y* values on the graph by the value of *a* (a stretch in the y-axis)

f(x) = sin(x)

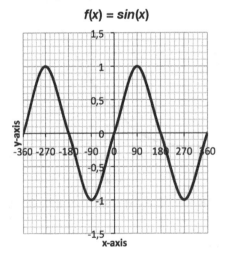

f(x) = 2sin(x)

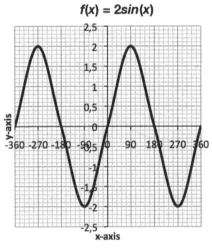

f(x + a)   Shifts the entire graph to the left by *a* units. For this example, let a = 180° so that a visible difference between the two graphs can be seen:

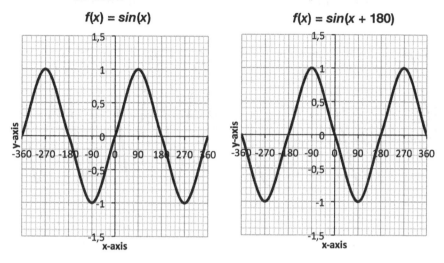

f(x − a)   Shifts the entire graph to the right by *a* units. Using a = 180° again:

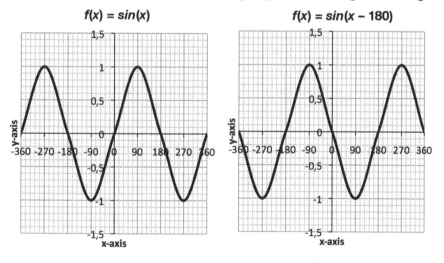

f(ax)   Stretches the x axis by a scale factor of $\frac{1}{a}$. Using a = 2:

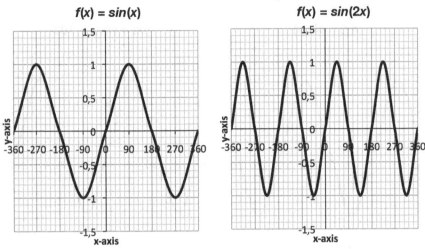

END OF CHAPTER QUESTIONS
(GRAPH TRANSFORMATIONS)

1. The dashed curve below has the equation y = f(x) and is translated so that the point at (0, 0) is mapped onto the point (0, –5).

Find an equation of the solid, translated curve below.

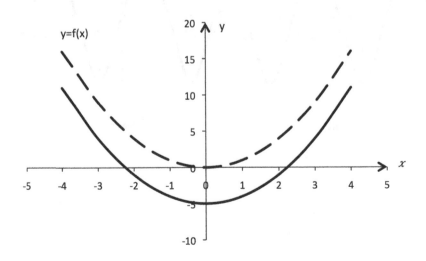

2. The grid below shows the graph of $y = sin(x)$ for values of x from −360 to 360.

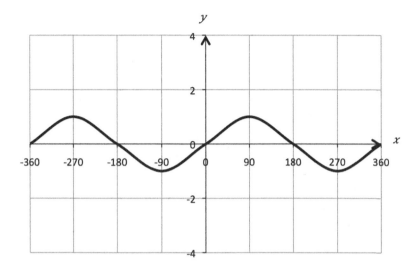

a) In words, describe the transformation $y=2sin(2x)$

b) On the grid below, sketch the graph of $y=2sin(2x)$ for values of x from −360 *to* 360.

3. If a curve, $f(x)$, is shifted 8 units to the left, what is the equation of the transformed curve?

CHAPTER 26:
TRIGONOMETRY

PYTHAGORAS THEOREM

This is a right angled triangle:

The side opposite the right angle is called the 'hypotenuse' and is the longest side of a right angled triangle

The side opposite an angle is, quite appropriately named 'opposite'

Right angle

Angle

The side that is not opposite the angle or the right angle in a right angled triangle is named 'adjacent'

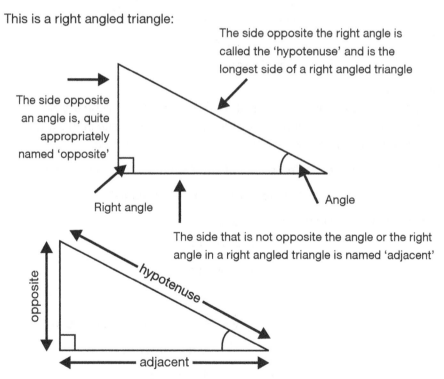

It is possible to calculate the length of a missing side on a right angled triangle if the other two sides are known, using Pythagoras theorem:

$$hypotenuse^2 = adjacent^2 + opposite^2$$

A useful tip when dealing with pythagoras theorem questions is that if you accidently confuse the opposite and adjacent sides with each other, it will make no difference to the final answer. The most important part is getting the hypotenuse correct.

EXAMPLE

Here is a right angled triangle. Calculate the value of y

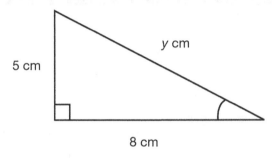

Diagram NOT accurately drawn

SOLUTION

I must first establish which side is the hypotenuse. This will be the side directly opposite the right angle labelled y cm. The opposite in this triangle is 5 cm (directly opposite the angle) and the adjacent is 8 cm.

Now that I know this, I refer to the Pythagoras theorem formula which is:

$$hypotenuse^2 = adjacent^2 + opposite^2$$

Substituting in the known values, I get:

$$y^2 = 8^2 + 5^2$$

$$y^2 = 64 + 25$$

$$y^2 = 89$$

$$y = \sqrt{89} \text{ (I used a calculator here)}$$

$$= 9.43 \text{ (to 2 decimal places)}$$

Therefore, the length $y = 9.43$ cm

EXAMPLE

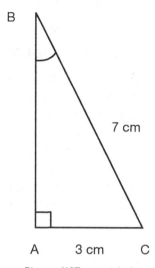

A   3 cm   C

Diagram NOT accurately drawn

ABC is a right-angled triangle.

AC= 3 cm

BC= 7 cm

Work out the length of AB. Give your answer correct to 3 significant figures.

SOLUTION

I know that the hypotenuse, BC, is opposite the right angle, which has value of 7cm in this example. The 'opposite' is AC with a value of 3 cm and the adjacent is AB, which is what I need to find.

Using the formula:

$$\textbf{\textit{hypotenuse}}^2 = \textbf{\textit{adjacent}}^2 + \textbf{\textit{opposite}}^2$$

I can rewrite this formula so that it is specific to this question:

$$\textbf{\textit{BC}}^2 = \textbf{\textit{AB}}^2 + \textbf{\textit{AC}}^2$$

I can also rearrange this formula so that AB^2 is the subject of the formula because I am trying to find AB:

$$\textbf{\textit{AB}}^2 = \textbf{\textit{BC}}^2 - \textbf{\textit{AC}}^2$$

I can now substitute in the values I already know, and I can even write :

$$\textbf{\textit{AB}}^2 = \textbf{7}^2 - \textbf{3}^2$$

$$AB^2 = 49 - 9$$

$$AB^2 = 40$$

$$AB = \sqrt{40} = 6.32\vdots45555 \text{ (using a calculator)}$$

Correct to 3 significant figures means cutting the number off just after the first three digits which are greater than zero (dotted line above). So in this case, for the number 6.324555, 3 significant figures would be 6.33 because I 'cut' between 2 and 4, and the number after the 4 is a 5, which means the 4 gets rounded up to a 5. Now, because the 4 has become a 5, this means the number that is before it (number 2) also gets rounded up, which is why the number 2 has become a 3. Remember that when rounding up, if a number in front is a 5 or more, the number before it always gets rounded up.

USING SIN, COS AND TAN

In the examples above, 2 lengths of a right-angled triangle are given, which makes it easy to find the third length. However, what if I was only given one length and asked to calculate the other lengths of a right-angled triangle, or what if I was given two lengths of a triangle and asked to calculate the internal angles?. This is where sin, cos and tan become useful.

EXAMPLE

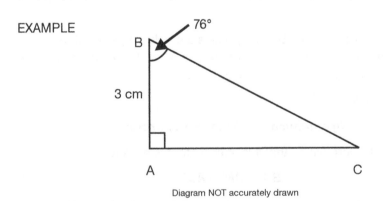

Diagram NOT accurately drawn

ABC is a right-angled triangle.

AB = 3 cm

Angle B = 76°

Work out the length of BC. Give your answer correct to 3 significant figures.

SOLUTION
(When a question says something like angle ABC, it is the middle letter which contains the angle)

For this triangle:

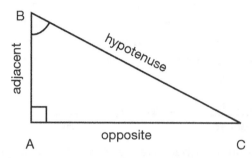

I now need to use the two quantities which I already know, which are the length AB and the angle B. I cannot use the Pythagoras theorem formula as I did in the previous examples as I have one length and one angle. The only way forward is to make use of sin, cos and tan.

Make sure you memorise SOH CAH TOA (pronounced 'socca toah'). The S, C and T stand for Sin, Cos and Tan respectively and the A, H and O stand for Adjacent, Hypotenuse and Opposite respectively. The relationships are shown below:

$$Sin\theta = \frac{opposite}{hypotenuse} \text{ (SOH)}$$

$$Cos\theta = \frac{adjacent}{hypotenuse} \text{ (CAH)}$$

$$Tan\theta = \frac{opposite}{adjacent} \text{ (TOA)}$$

To solve this question I need to select one of the above relationships so that I can substitute in the angle B and the length AB.

Length AB is the adjacent, which immediately prevents me from using $Sin\theta = \frac{opposite}{hypotenuse}$. This leaves me with two options, either the $Cos\theta$ or

Tanθ formulas. I now think of what the question is asking me. I need to find the length BC, which is the hypotenuse.

Therefore, I need one of the formulas above which allows me to substitute in the adjacent in order to find the hypotenuse i.e. a formula which contains both adjacent and hypotenuse. This would be $Cos\theta = \dfrac{adjacent}{hypotenuse}$. The symbol θ (pronounced 'theta') represents an angle and for this example, this would be angle B. To personalize the equation to this question, I can replace θ by the letter B, which would indicate I am working with the value of angle B and replace both adjacent and hypotenuse by their lengths AB and BC respectively:

$$Cos\theta = \frac{adjacent}{hypotenuse} \quad \longrightarrow \quad CosB = \frac{AB}{BC}$$

I can now substitute in what I already know into the equation, B = 76° and AB = 3 cm:

$$Cos76° = \frac{3}{BC}$$

Rearranging to make BC the subject of the equation:

$$BC = \frac{3}{Cos76°}$$

To calculate BC, I press 3 ÷ Cos76° into my calculator, which gives me:

BC = 3.639313328

Once again, the question requests the answer to be given to 3 significant figures. I therefore 'cut' (dotted line below) the number between the third and fourth digit:

BC = 3.63⋮9313328

The number directly after the dotted line is a 9, which means the number which precedes it gets rounded up. Therefore, the answer to 3 significant figures is:

BC = 3.64 cm

EXAMPLE

ABC is a right-angled triangle.

AB = 3 cm

BC = 5 cm

Calculate angle A in degrees showing all working out.

Diagram NOT accurately drawn

C

5 cm

A   3 cm   B

SOLUTION

I cannot use the Pythagoras theorem formula as the question asks to calculate an angle. This means I must use one of the three sin, cos and tan formulas given in the previous example.

To begin with, I need to know which sides of triangle ABC are the hypotenuse, opposite and adjacent so that I will be able to determine exactly which formula I can use. Remember that, the side opposite the right angle is the hypotenuse, and the side opposite the angle is called 'opposite' and the remaining side is the 'adjacent':

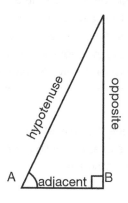

AB = 3 cm is the 'adjacent' and BC = 5 cm is the 'opposite' and because these are the only two lengths given in the question, it means I need a formula containing adjacent and opposite. This formula is:

$$\text{Tan}\,\theta = \frac{\text{opposite}}{\text{adjacent}} \text{ (TOA)}$$

As done in the previous example, I can personalise this equation to make it specific to this question. The symbol 'theta' θ can be replaced by the letter A, to indicate the fact I am trying to calculate angle A in the triangle above. Opposite and adjacent can be replaced by BC and AB respectively:

$$\text{Tan}A = \frac{BC}{AB}$$

I can now substitute the values for BC and AB into the formula:

$$\text{Tan}A = \frac{5}{3}$$

$$\text{Tan}A = 1.666666 \text{ ... ...}$$

$$A = \text{tan}^{-1}1.66666666 \text{ ...}$$

$$A = 59°$$

To arrive at this answer using a calculator, first type in the initial division of 5 divided by 3. Once the answer to this is on the calculator screen, which should now read 1.6666666.... press the shift key and immediately after this press the 'tan' button to give 59.036...

The above examples illustrate the type of questions you are likely to be faced with in a GCSE maths exam involving right-angled triangles. Try the end of chapter questions for practice.

END OF CHAPTER QUESTIONS:
(PYTHAGORAS THEOREM AND THE USE OF SIN, COS
AND TAN IN RIGHT ANGLED TRIANGLES)

1.

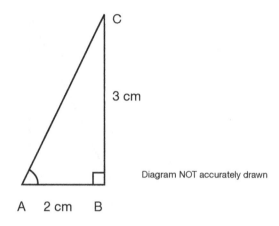

Diagram NOT accurately drawn

ABC is a right angled triangle. AB = 2 cm and BC = 3 cm

    a) Calculate the length AC.

    b) Calculate the angle A. Give your answer to 3 significant figures

2. Triangle ABC is a right angled triangle. AB = 10 cm and BC = 5 cm

    a) Calculate the length AC.

    b) Calculate the angle A. Give your answer to 3 significant figures

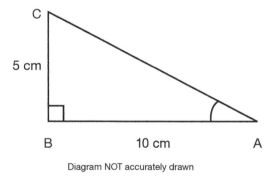

Diagram NOT accurately drawn

3. ABC is a right angled triangle. AB = 2 cm and angle C = 35°.
Calculate the length AC. Show all working out, giving your answer to
3 significant figures.

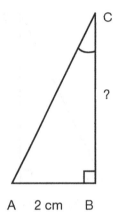

Diagram NOT accurately drawn

CHAPTER 27:
USING SIN, COS AND TAN IN TRIANGLES THAT ARE NOT RIGHT ANGLED

SINE RULE

For a triangle that is not right angled, the sine rule is useful providing that at least 2 sides and an angle of the triangle are known or 2 angles and 1 side of the triangle are known.

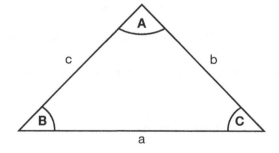

The sine rule is given by:

$$\frac{a}{sin\mathbf{A}} = \frac{b}{sin\mathbf{B}}$$

Where the small letters represent lengths and the capital letters represent angles.

The sine rule formula is usually printed on the inside of the front cover in the exam booklets, so you do not have to memorise it.

*** Note that before starting this chapter, it is worth checking that your calculator is in degree mode ***

EXAMPLE

For the triangle shown below, calculate the missing length y

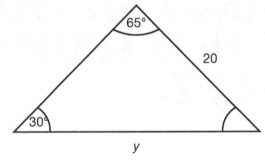

Diagram NOT accurately drawn

SOLUTION

There are 2 angles and one side provided, which means I can use the sine rule.

$$\frac{a}{sin\mathbf{A}} = \frac{b}{sin\mathbf{B}}$$

Remember that capital letters are angles and small letters are lengths. A small letter's corresponding capital letter e.g. a and A are always opposite each other which makes knowing which numbers to put into the sine rule a lot easier:

The length 20 is opposite 30°: $\dfrac{20}{sin30°}$

The length y is opposite 65°: $\dfrac{y}{sin65°}$

I can now equate the two:

$$\frac{20}{sin30°} = \frac{y}{sin65°}$$

Rearranging:

$$y = \frac{20sin65°}{sin30°}$$

Using a calculator, I can now calculate the value of y:

$$y = \frac{20sin65°}{sin30°} = 36.25$$

To calculate this I typed 20*sin*65÷sin30 into a calculator followed by the equals sign.

EXAMPLE
Find the missing length of the triangle, x

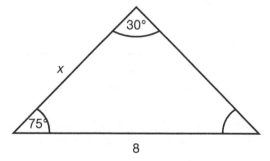

Diagram NOT accurately drawn

SOLUTION
Once again, there are 2 angles and one side provided. However, the angle opposite the length x I am trying to find is unknown, which means I cannot use the sine rule unless I establish what the missing angle is first.

I can do this because I know that all angles in a triangle add up to 180°, so to find the missing angle I can subtract the two known angles from 180°:

Missing angle = 180° – 75° – 30° = 75°

Now that I know the angle opposite the length x is 75° I can use the sine rule to find x:

$$\frac{x}{sin75°} = \frac{8}{sin30°}$$

$$x = \frac{8sin75°}{sin30°} = 15.46 \text{ (2 decimal places)}$$

The sine rule can also be used to calculate a missing angle from a triangle, as demonstrated in the example below.

EXAMPLE
Find the value of the missing angle, $Z°$, in the triangle below

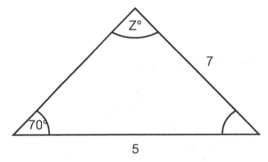

Diagram NOT accurately drawn

SOLUTION
I have 2 sides and one angle. Both lengths are directly opposite their corresponding opposite angle, 7 is opposite 70° and 5 is opposite $Z°$ which means I can use the sine rule:

$$\frac{5}{sinZ°} = \frac{7}{sin70°}$$

I now need to isolate $SinZ°$:

$$sinZ° = \frac{5 \times sin70°}{7}$$

$$sinZ° = 0.671209014$$

To find z° I now press the following buttons in the order shown:

Shift, sin, 0.671209014, equals and I get 42.16°

Written down, the buttons pressed on the calculator are equivalent to:

$$Z° = sin^{-1}0.671209014$$

$$\mathbf{Z = 42.16°}$$

COSINE RULE AND CALCULATING THE AREA OF A TRIANGLE

The sine rule could only be used if the length and the angle were directly opposite each other. Consider the following triangle:

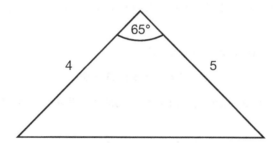

The cosine rule provides an alternative method if the length and angle are not opposite each other as is the situation for the above triangle.

The cosine rule is given by:

Cosine Rule $a^2 = b^2 + c^2 - 2bc \, cosA$

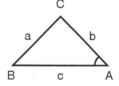

To calculate the area of a triangle that is not right angled, the following formula is used (given in the exam booklet):

Area of triangle $= \frac{1}{2} ab \, sinC$

EXAMPLE

Find the missing length, a, in the triangle below

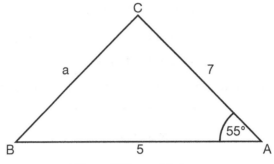

Diagram NOT accurately drawn

SOLUTION

There are 2 lengths given, which are opposite angles B and C, both of which are not given in the question. This means that the cosine rule needs to be used. Another tip for knowing when to use the cosine rule is to see if an angle is surrounded by two lengths either side of it, as is the case in the above triangle.

Cosine Rule $a^2 = b^2 + c^2 - 2bc \, cosA$

$$b = 7, c = 5 \text{ and } A = 55°$$

To find the missing length, a, I need to substitute the above into the cosine rule:

$$a^2 = 7^2 + 5^2 - 2 \times 7 \times 5 \times cos55°$$

$$a^2 = 49 + 25 - 70 \times cos55°$$

$$a^2 = 74 - 70 \times cos55°$$

$$a^2 = 74 - 40.15035054$$

$$a^2 = 33.84964946$$

$$a^2 = \sqrt{33.84964946} = 5.818 = 5.82$$

The value of the length a is 5.82

EXAMPLE
In triangle ABC,

AC = 7 cm
BC = 9 cm
Angle ACB = 64°

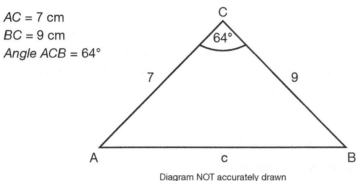

Diagram NOT accurately drawn

a) Calculate the area of triangle ABC. Give your answer correct to 3 significant figures.

b) Calculate the length of AB. Give your answer correct to 3 significant figures.

SOLUTION
a) To calculate an area of a triangle that is not right-angled, the following formula is used:

Area of triangle $= \dfrac{1}{2} ab\ sinC$

$$a = 7, b = 9 \text{ and } C = 64°$$

I can substitute these values into the area of triangle formula:

Area of triangle $= \dfrac{1}{2} \times 7 \times 9 \times sin64°$

Area of triangle = 28.3 cm² (3 significant figures)

Remember that the letter C is just used to indicate that the angle which needs to be used in the 'area of triangle' formula should be a different letter from the two lengths. This means that the formula could also be written as, depending on which letter the angle is on:

Area of triangle $= \dfrac{1}{2} ac\ sinB \text{ or } \dfrac{1}{2} bc\ sinA$

This formula will always work as long as an angle has two lengths either side of it. It really doesn't matter which sides of the triangle are labelled A, B or C.

b) To calculate the length AB I must use the cosine rule, however, I do not know the angle A, but I do know the angle C, which means I can swap A with C. Doing this means I must also swap the corresponding small letters, a with c and c with a:

The 'old' cosine rule:

Cosine Rule $a^2 = b^2 + c^2 - 2bc\ cosA$

The 'new' cosine rule for this question:

Cosine Rule $c^2 = b^2 + a^2 - 2ba\ cosC$

I can now substitute in the values I already know: $a = 7$, $b = 9$ and $C = 64°$

$$c^2 = 9^2 + 7^2 - 2 \times 9 \times 7 \times cos64°$$

$$c^2 = 81 + 49 - 55.2347645$$

$$c^2 = 130 - 55.234765$$

$$c^2 = 74.7652355$$

$$c = \sqrt{74.7652355} = 8.65 \text{ (3 significant figures)}$$

Therefore, length AB is 8.65 cm

EXAMPLE
In triangle ABC,

$AB = 7$ cm
$BC = 9$ cm
Angle $ABC = 64°$

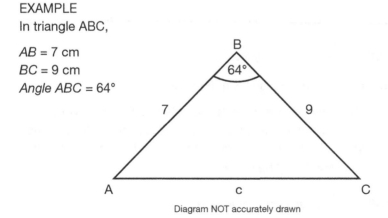

Diagram NOT accurately drawn

Calculate the area of triangle ABC. Give your answer correct to 3 significant figures.

SOLUTION

Although the numbers are the same in this example compared to the previous one, the letters on the triangle are different.

This example aims to demonstrate how to deal with the area of triangle formula with an angle which is not labelled C.

The area of a triangle that is not right-angled is given by:

$$\textbf{Area of triangle} = \frac{1}{2} ab\, sinC$$

However, I do not know the angle C. What I do know is the angle B. So what I can do is replace the letter C in the equation with the letter B and replace the small *b* with a small *c*. The equation now looks like:

$$\textbf{Area of triangle} = \frac{1}{2} ac\, sinB$$

$$a = 7, c = 9\ and\ B = 64°$$

Substituting these into the 'area of triangle' formula gives:

$$\textbf{Area of triangle} = \frac{1}{2} \times 7 \times 9 \times sin64°$$

$$\textbf{Area of triangle} = 28.3\ cm^2\ (3\ significant\ figures)$$

EXAMPLE
In triangle ABC,

AB = 7 cm
BC = 9 cm
AC = 11 cm

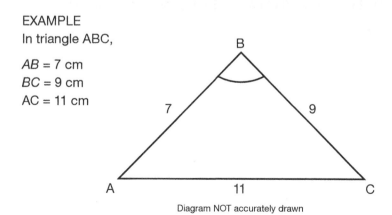

Diagram NOT accurately drawn

Calculate the angle B. Give your answer to 3 significant figures.

SOLUTION

I have 3 lengths and no angles. This combination is perfect for the cosine rule. However, I am interested in angle B and not angle A, which is what the standard cosine rule formula uses:

Cosine Rule $a^2 = b^2 + c^2 - 2bc\ cosA$

As shown in previous examples, I need to 'swap' the letters A and B and at the same time 'swap' the corresponding small letters a and b which now makes the cosine rule formula:

Cosine Rule $b^2 = a^2 + c^2 - 2ac\ cosB$

I can now substitute into this formula $a = 9$ cm, $b = 11$ cm and $c = 7$ cm

$$11^2 = 9^2 + 7^2 - 2 \times 9 \times 7 \times cosB$$

$$121 = 81 + 49 - 126 \times cosB$$

$$121 = 130 - 126cosB$$

$$121 - 130 = -126cosB$$

$$-9 = -126cosB$$

$$-9 \div (-126) = cosB$$

$$cosB = 0.071428571$$

To solve for B, press shift on the calculator followed by the cos button, then type in 0.071428571 and finally press equals to get:

B = cos⁻¹0.071428571 = 85.90395624° = 85.9° (3 significant figures)

The angle B is 85.9°

END OF CHAPTER QUESTIONS
(USING SIN, COS AND TAN IN TRIANGLES THAT ARE
NOT RIGHT ANGLED)

1.

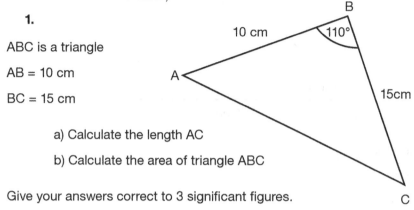

ABC is a triangle

AB = 10 cm

BC = 15 cm

a) Calculate the length AC

b) Calculate the area of triangle ABC

Give your answers correct to 3 significant figures.

2.

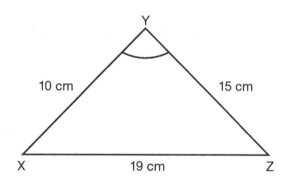

XYZ is a triangle

XY = 10 cm

XZ = 25 cm

YZ = 15 cm

Calculate the angle XYZ, giving your answer to 2 decimal places.

3.

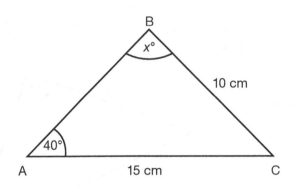

ABC is a triangle.

ABC = $x°$

BAC = 60°

AC = 15 cm

BC = 7 cm

Calculate the value of angle X, giving your answer correct to 2 decimal places.

CHAPTER 28:
PERCENTAGES

Percentages are used in everyday situations, some of which are listed below:

- Value added tax (V.A.T) currently added to all transactions in the UK at 17.5%

- Discounts in shops where a certain percentage off the listed price is offered e.g. 20% off a pair of jeans.

- Depreciation of items, typically cars e.g. a car depreciates in value by 12% per annum.

- And many more...

This chapter aims to make you feel at ease when faced with percentage calculations. Follow the examples carefully and you will have no problems dealing with percentages at the end of this chapter. You can test your understanding with the end of chapter practice questions.

Before the examples begin, it is worth going through two essential formulas when working with percentages: percentage increase and decrease formulas (see below)

$$\% \ increase = \frac{highest \ value - lowest \ value}{lowest \ value}$$

$$\% \ decrease = \frac{highest\ value - lowest\ value}{highest\ value}$$

Because these two formulas are so similar, it is easy to confuse the % increase formula with the % decrease one. This is why I have given you a useful tip below, which I personally use to remember the difference:

A USEFUL TIP

The answer for a % increase will be higher than the original value yet to find the % increase, the formula requires a division by the lowest value. Therefore, to remember this formula, always think that a % increase, which gives the **highest** value, must be divided by the **lowest** number.

For the % decrease formula, the opposite is true i.e. a % decrease gives the **lowest** value and it must be divided by the **highest** value.

EXAMPLE
There is currently a sale at a clothing store. Normal prices are reduced by 14%. The sale price of a cotton shirt is £43.

Work out the normal price of the cotton shirt

SOLUTION
Questions similar to this example will always appear in the calculator paper. I will therefore be going through this example in a way that explains how to use the calculator to answer it.

Put simply, I know that the cotton shirt has already been reduced by a percentage decrease of 14%, so in order for me to find the price before 14% was deducted, I need to increase the sale price given to me in the question by 14%. I can use the above formula for % decrease:

$$\% \ decrease = \frac{highest\ value - lowest\ value}{highest\ value}$$

For this example all the information I currently have is:

% decrease = 14%
Lowest value = £43

I now substitute what I know into the formula:

$$14\% = \frac{\text{highest value} - £43}{\text{highest value}}$$

I now put '*highest value = x*' into the formula and convert 14% into a decimal:

$$0.14 = \frac{x - £43}{x}$$

• Remember that $14\% = \frac{14}{100} = 0.14$ and $x = $ *highest value*

I now multiply both sides of the equation by x:

$$0.14 \times x = \frac{x - £43}{x} \times x$$

The two x's on the right hand side cancel to leave:

$$0.14x = x - £43$$

Next step is to bring all the x's to one side:

$$0.14x - x = -£43$$

I can now subtract the x terms (using a calculator, I typed in 0.14−1= −0.86):

$$-0.86x = -£43$$

I now need to isolate x to get the final answer. The two negatives cancel each other out (below in bold):

$$x = \frac{-£43}{-0.86} = £50$$

Remember that $x = $ highest value

Because $x = £50$, this means that the highest value i.e. original price of the jacket was £50.

EXAMPLE

Susan earns £500 a week after a pay rise of 10%. How much did she earn before the pay rise?

SOLUTION

Susan now earns 10% more than she did before. In other words, her pay has increased by 10% and therefore, this is the percentage increase. Knowing this, I can use the % increase formula given at the start of this chapter:

$$\% \text{ increase} = \frac{\text{highest value} - \text{lowest value}}{\text{lowest value}}$$

For this example, all the information I currently have is:

% increase = 10%
Highest value = £500

Also, let x = lowest value for this equation

I can now substitute the above into the % increase equation:

$$10\% = \frac{£500 - x}{x}$$

- Remember that $10\% = \frac{10}{100} = 0.1$

I now multiply both sides of the equation by x:

$$0.1 \times x = \frac{£500 - x}{x} \times x$$

The two x's on the right hand side cancel to leave:

$$0.1x = £500 - x$$

Next step is to bring all the x's to one side:

$$0.1x + x = £500$$

I can now add the x terms (using a calculator, I typed in 0.1 + 1 = 1.1):

$$1.1x = £500$$

I now need to isolate x to get the final answer:

$$x = \frac{£500}{1.1} = £454.545454...$$

Rounding this to two decimal places, the answer is £454.55

Remember that x = lowest value

Because x = £454.55, this means that the lowest value i.e. Susan's original earnings was £454.55.

HOW TO CHECK THE ANSWER IS CORRECT (WITHOUT SEEING THE ANSWERS!)

Now that I have Susan's original pay and her pay after the 10% increase, if I increase the answer I have arrived at, £454.55 by 10% I should get an answer of £500.

Susan's pay before the pay rise is £454.55

To increase this by 10% I use the % increase formula, because I need to increase this value by 10%:

$$\% \text{ increase} = \frac{\text{highest value} - \text{lowest value}}{\text{lowest value}}$$

If you work your way through this, substituting in:

% increase = 10% and

Lowest value = £454.55

You will arrive at an answer of £500. This proves that my answer is correct.

EXAMPLE
A department store increases the price of furniture by 30% in July. In November, it decreases the price of furniture by 30%. Will the July price be the same as the November price for furniture? Show all working out.

SOLUTION
Although it seems like the price went up by 30% then came down by 30% to make it exactly what it was before the increase, this is not the case.

The way to tackle this question is to use a number and see what happens when I increase and decrease the chosen number by 30%. I will use the number 100 because it's an easy number to work with:

Although not stated in the question, assume that the price of furniture before July is £100. The question states that in July there is an increase of 30% in the price of furniture. I must now use the percentage increase formula with £100 being the lowest value and 30% being the % increase:

$$\% \text{ increase} = \frac{\text{highest value} - \text{lowest value}}{\text{lowest value}}$$

$$30\% = \frac{\text{highest value} - £100}{£100}$$

I need to convert 30% into a decimal before continuing:

$$30\% = \frac{30}{100} = \frac{3}{10} = 0.3$$

Now the equation is:

$$0.3 = \frac{\text{highest value} - £100}{£100}$$

Multiplying both sides by £100:

$$0.3 \times £100 = \frac{\text{highest value} - £100}{£100} \times £100$$

The two £100's cancel on the right hand side of the equation which leaves:

$$0.3 \times £100 = \text{highest value} - £100$$

Multiplying the left hand side:

$$£30 = \text{highest value} - £100$$

To isolate 'highest value', I need to bring the £100 on the right to the left of the equation:

$$£30 + £100 = \text{highest value}$$

$$\text{highest value} = £130$$

This means that after an increase of 30%, if the furniture cost £100, it now costs £130. Therefore, the June price is £130.

The question now states that the price is reduced by 30% in November. 'The price' refers to the price from July onwards i.e. £130. Because it is a decrease, I can use the % decrease formula with highest value being £130 and % decrease being 30%:

$$\% \ decrease = \frac{highest\ value - lowest\ value}{highest\ value}$$

$$30\% = \frac{£130 - lowest\ value}{£130}$$

From previously, I know 30% = 0.3

$$0.3 = \frac{£130 - lowest\ value}{£130}$$

Multiplying both sides of the equation by £130:

$$0.3 \times £130 = \frac{£130 - lowest\ value}{£130} \times £130$$

Both £130's on the right hand side of the equation cancel each other out, leaving:

$$0.3 \times £130 = £130 - lowest\ value$$

$$£39 = £130 - lowest\ value$$

Isolating the 'lowest value' term:

$$£39 - £130 = -lowest\ value$$

$$-£91 = -lowest\ value$$

The two negative signs cancel each other to leave:

$$£91 = lowest\ value$$

This means that the price of furniture after the reduction of 30% in November is £91, assuming that furniture cost before July is £100.

Therefore, to answer the original question asked, the price of furniture in July is not the same as the price of furniture in November for the above reasons.

Put simply, when the price is increased by 30% the price became a larger figure compared to the original price. Because the price is now a larger figure, any percentage taken off this larger price would mean a larger amount gets taken off. So, when the price must be decreased by 30%, it is 30% off a larger number which would lead to a larger amount being taken off.

Think of it as a discount in a store. Let's say the store is offering 30% off any item. You will get a greater discount if you buy something that is more money compared to an item that is cheaper, see for yourself next time you're out shopping!

EXAMPLE

A laptop costs £420 plus 17.5% VAT.

What is the total cost of the laptop?

SOLUTION

I need to increase £420 by 17.5%. Because I need to increase a quantity I can use the % increase formula:

$$\% \text{ increase} = \frac{\text{highest value} - \text{lowest value}}{\text{lowest value}}$$

Where

$$\% \text{ increase} = 17.5\% = \frac{17.5}{100} = 0.175$$

Lowest value = £420

I now substitute the above into the % increase formula:

$$0.175 = \frac{\text{highest value} - £420}{£420}$$

Next, I multiply both sides by £420:

$$0.175 \times £420 = \frac{\text{highest value} - £420}{£420} \times £420$$

$$0.175 \times £420 = \text{highest value} - £420$$

$$£73.5 = \text{highest value} - £420$$

$$£73.5 + £420 = \text{highest value}$$

$$£493.5 = \text{highest value}$$

The highest value is £493.5, which means that the cost of the laptop with VAT added on is 493 pounds and 50 pence.

EXAMPLE

James invested £2000 for n years in a bank.

He was paid 2% per annum compound interest.

At the end of n years, James had £2080.80 from the bank.

Work out the value of n

SOLUTION

When asked to find the number of years of investment, it is quickest and easiest to use the formula:

$$Total\ amount\ after\ n\ years = Original\ amount \times (1+ \frac{\%interest}{100})^n$$

So, for this example, the formula becomes:

$$£2080.80 = £2000 \times (1+ \frac{2}{100})^n$$

$$£2080.80 = £2000 \times (1 + 0.02)^n$$

$$£2080.80 = £2000 \times (1.02)^n$$

$$\frac{£2080.80}{£2000} = (1.02)^n$$

$$£1.0404 = (1.02)^n$$

There is no way to find the value of n apart from trial and error now. The only way is to plug in the number 1.02 and press the 'to the power of' button on your calculator and try a few numbers, starting with 2 onwards. The answer is n = 2 in this case, which means that it took 2 years for the money to rise to £2080.80 from the bank

END OF CHAPTER QUESTIONS (PERCENTAGES)

1. A man invests £2000 for 2 years in a bank. The bank paid him 2% compound interest per annum (every year).

   a) After the first year, how much money did the man have in the bank?

   b) At the end of the second year, how much did the man have in the bank?

2. Jack invests £3000 into a bank savings account. He was paid 8% compound interest per annum. At the end of n years, Jack found he has £3499.20 in his savings account.

Work out the value of n

3. A TV costs £500 plus 17.5% VAT.

What is the total cost of the TV?

4. The value of a new car is £7000. The car's value depreciates by 20% each year.

Work out the value of the car at the end of 3 years.

CHAPTER 29:
EXCHANGE RATES, VALUE FOR MONEY AND TIME TO EMPTY A TANK PROBLEMS

For GCSE mathematics, you may be asked to convert currencies from one to another or find which of two containers e.g. large or small gives better value for money or calculate the time it takes to empty a container given some information on the rate it empties. This chapter will provide you with a neat and easy way of doing all of this.

EXAMPLE

A group of friends travelled to France for their holidays and they each changed £420 into Euros.

The exchange rate was £1 = €1.20

      a) Change £420 into Euros (€)

The group return home and gather all their remaining cash. They change

€320 Euros into pounds.

The new exchange rate was £1= €1.10

  b) Change €320 into pounds

SOLUTION

The way I tackle these types of questions are as follows:

a)

The question tells me that £1 gives me €1.20, so to get £420 I need to multiply this by €1.20.

I usually write out what I know in this form, note that I align £1 and £420 underneath each other:

  £1 gives €1.20

  £420 gives x

To find how many Euros x is, cross multiplication is used as follows:

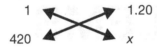

Carrying out the cross multiplication:

$$1 \times x = 1.20 \times 420$$

$$x = 1.20 \times 420$$

$$x = €504$$

Therefore x = €504 which means that £420 gives €504

b)

I am given a new exchange rate for part b) of £1= €1.60. Calculating the exchange will take the same form as a):

  £1 gives €1.60

  x gives £320

Where x is the number of pounds that give €320 at the exchange rate of £1= €1.60

To calculate x, I need to cross multiply as I did in part a):

£1 $\quad\quad$ €1.60

x $\quad\quad$ €320

$$1 \times 320 = 1.60 \times x$$

$$320 = 1.60x$$

$$x = 320 \div 1.60$$

$$x = £200$$

Therefore, the group will get £200 when they exchange their €320 at the new exchange rate which was £1 = €1.60

Other examples where this method can be used to solve the problem are given below.

EXAMPLE

A box of flour is sold in two sizes: Medium and Large.

A medium box contains 4 kg of flour and costs £2.40

A large box contains 6kg of flour and costs £5.70

Which size of box gives the best value for money?

Explain your answer, showing all working out.

SOLUTION

When approached with such a question, I always find the price per kg and the cheapest out of the two is the better value for money. In order to find the price per kg for both boxes, I need to do some cross multiplication:

Medium box calculation

4 kg   costs   £2.40

1 kg   costs x

x is the cost of 1kg of flour for the medium box

Cross multiplying:

$$4 \times x = 2.40 \times 1$$
$$4x = 2.40$$
$$x = 2.40 \div 4$$
$$x = £0.6 = 60p$$

Therefore 1kg costs 60p for the medium box i.e. 60p per kg (60p/kg).

Large box calculation

$$6 \text{ kg} \quad \text{costs} \quad £5.70$$
$$1 \text{ kg} \quad \text{costs} \quad x$$

x is the cost of 1kg of flour for the large box.

Cross multiplying:

6 kg ⤫ £5.70
1 kg ⤫ x

$$6 \times x = 5.70 \times 1$$
$$6x = 5.70$$
$$x = 5.70 \div 6$$
$$x = £0.95 = 95p$$

Therefore 1kg costs 95p for the large box i.e. 95p per kg (90p/kg)

Comparing the medium and large boxes, it is clear that the medium box offers better value for money as it is cheaper per kg at 60p compared to the large box which costs 90p for the same amount.

EXAMPLE

There are 30 litres of liquid in a tank.

The liquid flows out of the tank at a rate of 100 millilitres per second.

1 litre = 1000 millilitres

Calculate the time it takes for the barrel to empty completely.

SOLUTION

I firstly need to convert 100 millilitres into litres. I know that:

$$1 \text{ litre} \quad \text{is equivalent to} \quad 1000 \text{ millilitres}$$

$$x \text{ litre} \quad \text{is equivalent to} \quad 100 \text{ millilitres}$$

I now need to find x, and I can do this through cross multiplication:

$$1 \text{ litre} \qquad 1000 \text{ millilitres}$$

$$x \text{ litres} \qquad 100 \text{ millilitres}$$

$$1 \times 100 = x \times 1000$$

$$100 = 1000x$$

$$x = 100 \div 1000 = 0.1$$

This means that 0.1 litres is equivalent to 100 millilitres. It also means that the rate at which the tank empties is 0.1 litres per second. I now know the following:

0.1 litres leave the barrel every 1 second

To find how long it would take to empty a 30 litre tank completely, I use cross multiplication once again. I will call the time to empty the tank completely y:

0.1 litres leave every **1** second

30 litres leave every **y** seconds

$$0.1 \text{ litres} \qquad 1 \text{ second}$$

$$30 \text{ litres} \qquad x \text{ seconds}$$

$$0.1 \times y = 30 \times 1$$

$$0.1y = 30$$

$$y = 30 \div 0.1 = 300 \text{ secondes} = 5 \text{ minutes}$$

The amount of time required to empty all 30 litres of the tank completely is 300 seconds or 5 minutes.

END OF CHAPTER QUESTIONS (EXCHANGE RATES, VALUE FOR MONEY AND TIME TO EMPTY TANK PROBLEMS)

1. The current exchange rate is £1 = €1.05
   What will someone who converts £310 into Euros get using the current exchange rate?

2. A car has covered 120 miles using 30 litres of fuel. If 1 litre of fuel costs £1.19 calculate how much it would cost to travel 320 miles using the same car.

3. A 120 litre capacity barrel fills up at the rate of 1 litre per second. How long will the barrel take to fill?

4. A 120 litre barrel fills up at the rate of 0.5 litres per second. How long will the barrel take to fill?

5. At the supermarket, a pack of 10 cans of fizzy drink costs £5 and a pack of 5 cans of fizzy drink cost £3, which of the two offer best value for money?.

Show all working out.

CHAPTER 30:
UPPER AND LOWER BOUNDS

In the exam, you may be given a quantity and told to specify the largest possible amount the quantity could possibly be or alternatively the smallest amount the quantity could be, or both. This chapter examines how to do this through the use of examples, with practice questions to try at the end.

EXAMPLE

A ruler is 30 cm in length, correct to the nearest centimetre.

   a) What is the greatest possible length of the ruler

   b) What is the smallest possible length of the ruler

SOLUTION

   a) The greatest possible length of the ruler is 30.5 cm, anything above 30.5 get's rounded up to 31cm. For example, 30.6 get's rounded up to 31 cm and therefore cannot be the greatest possible length, only 30.5 cm can.

   b) The smallest possible length of the ruler is 29.5 cm, which if rounded up, becomes 30cm. If the number is less than 29.5 cm, for example 29.4 cm then it is rounded down to 29 cm, therefore 29.5 cm is the smallest possible length the ruler can be.

EXAMPLE
Find the upper and lower bounds of 15.24

SOLUTION
The quantity 15.24 consists of two decimal places. In this case, I need to look at the very last number, which is the number 4. I now need to consider the upper and lower bounds of the number 4 only:

Upper bound (the greatest possible number 4 can be) = 4.5

Lower bound (the smallest possible number 4 can be) = 3.5

The trick is to now ignore the decimal places, and place the number 45 in place of the number 4 in the number 15.24, which will give me the upper bound of the number 15.24:

Upper bound of 15.24= 15.245

The same applies for the lower bound, ignore the decimal place and replace the number 4 on 15.24 with 35:

Lower bound of 15.24 = 15.235

EXAMPLE
A 100m sprint takes a runner 15 seconds. Calculate:

a) The upper bound of the runner's average speed

b) The lower bound of the runner's average speed

Write down all figures on your calculator display.

SOLUTION

$$Average\ speed = \frac{distance}{time}$$

a) To calculate the upper bound of the runner's average speed, I need to know the upper bound of the distance and the lower bound of the time.

The reason I will use the lower bound of time and not upper bound of time is because the larger the number that is doing the dividing, the smaller the answer will be and I need the largest possible answer in this case for average speed (upper bound of average speed).

Explanation – not part of the solution to the example

Can you see, for example, that if I divide $\frac{4}{2} = 2$, but if I now use a number lower than 2, let's say 1, on the bottom half of the fraction and keep the top of the fraction the same, then I get a larger answer? $\frac{4}{1} = 4$. This is the same principle used to answer this question. I need the largest possible value of average speed.

Upper bound of distance = 200.5 m

Lower bound of time = 14.5 seconds

$$\textbf{\textit{Upper bound of average speed}} = \frac{distance}{time} = \frac{200.5}{14.5} = 13.82758621$$

b) To calculate the lower bound of the runners average speed, I now need to use the lower bound of the distance and the upper bound of the time:

Lower bound of distance =199.5 m

Upper bound of time = 15.5 seconds

$$\textbf{\textit{Lower bound of average speed}} = \frac{distance}{time} = \frac{199.5}{15.5} = 12.87096774$$

END OF CHAPTER QUESTIONS
(UPPER AND LOWER BOUNDS)

1. A square has sides of 2.4 cm in length. Calculate:

    a) The lower bound of the area of the square

    b) The upper bound of the area of the square

2. Write the lower and upper bounds of 150.

3. The area of a rectangle is 240 cm². One side of the rectangle is 10 cm in length.

10 cm
x cm

Calculate:

    a) The upper bound of the length x

    b) The lower bound of the length x

Write down all the numbers displayed in your calculator.

CHAPTER 31: PROBABILITY

QUICK FACTS ABOUT PROBABILITY

Some events have a probability of 0; this means that the event is impossible and will never take place. A probability of 1 means the event is certain and will take place for sure. Other events have a probability between 0 and 1, with an event having a 50% chance of occurring when the probability is 0.5 i.e. between 0 and 1. Probabilities can be written as decimals, fractions and percentages.

Two events are independent if they have no influence on one another. For example, if I rolled a dice and it lands on 6 this will not have anything to do with my chances of winning the lottery i.e. the two events are independent.

To work out the probability of two independent events occurring, the AND rule can be used, which simply means multiplying the two probabilities:

$$P (A \text{ and } B) = P (A) \times P (B)$$

There is also an OR rule, which means adding the two probabilities:

$$P (A \text{ or } B) = P (A) + P (B)$$

The AND/OR rules are used often throughout this chapter and you will be notified of when they are being used.

EXAMPLE

Simon and Jane both sit the same GCSE maths paper.
The probability that Jane will pass the test is 0.8
The probability that Simon will pass the test is 0.6

a) Complete the probability tree diagram below

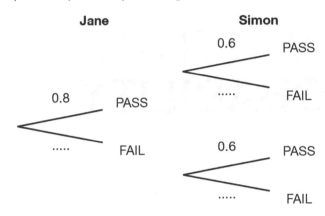

b) What is the probability that both Simon and Jane will both pass the GCSE exam?

c) What is the probability that only one of them will fail the GCSE exam paper?

d) What is the probability that at least one passes?

SOLUTION

a) I know that the branches, when added vertically must add up to 1:

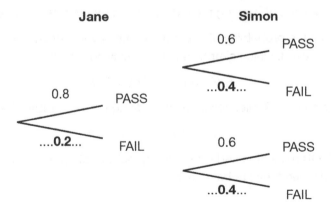

So, for Jane, 0.8 + *a number* = 1, to solve this I can simply calculate 1 − 0.8 to get the missing number:

$$1 - 0.8 = 0.2$$

For Simon, 0.6 + *a number* = 1 and to calculate 'a number' I subtract 0.6 from 1:

$$1 - 0.6 = 0.4$$

b) To find the probability of Jane and Simon both passing I need to follow the route along the probability tree of Jane passing then Simon passing. Using the AND rule, I will also be multiplying the numbers as I go along (in bold below):

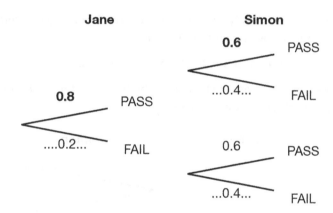

There are only two numbers to be multiplied on the 'pass pass' route:

$$P \text{ (Jane AND Simon both pass)} = 0.8 \times 0.6 = 0.48$$

The probability of Jane and Simon both passing is 0.48

c) To find the probability of only one of them failing the exam paper, I need to find all the possibilities on the probability tree where one fails and the other passes. There are two ways:

Jane can pass and Simon can fail OR Jane can fail and Simon can pass.

The first is shown below in bold (Jane passes, Simon fails):

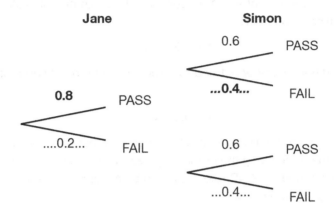

To calculate the probability of Jane passing and Simon failing I multiply the numbers in bold above using the AND rule:

P (Jane passes AND Simon fails) = 0.8 × 0.4 = 0.32

There is also another pass, fail route on the tree. This time Jane fails and Simon passes, shown in bold below:

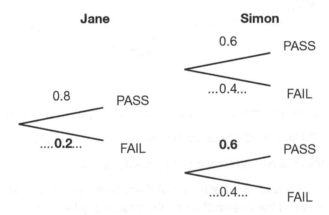

To calculate the probability of Jane failing and Simon passing, I multiply the numbers in italic using the AND rule:

P (Jane fails AND Simon passes) = 0.2 × 0.6 = 0.12

To find the total probability of only one of them failing the maths paper, I need to **add** the two results I have found above using the OR rule, because either Jane OR Simon can pass at any one time:

P (Jane passes and Simon fails OR Jane fails and Simon passes)
= 0.32 + 0.12 = 0.44

The probability of only one of them failing the maths paper is 0.44

EXAMPLE

In a game of tennis, a player can win, draw or lose.

Tim plays 2 games of tennis

The probability that Tim wins any game of tennis is 0.7
The probability that Tim loses any game of tennis is 0.2

 a) Complete the probability tree diagram below.

 b) Calculate the probability that Tim will draw both games

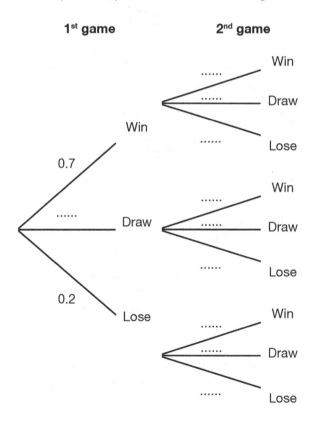

1ˢᵗ game   **2ⁿᵈ game**

SOLUTION

a) Remember that the probabilities on each branch, which contain 3 mini branches (win, draw, lose) must add up to a total of 1. Therefore, to find the value of 'P(draw)' the calculation is:

$$0.7 + 0.2 + P(draw) = 1$$

$$P(draw) = 1 - 0.7 - 0.2$$

$$P(draw) = 0.1$$

Now I can complete the probability tree diagram:

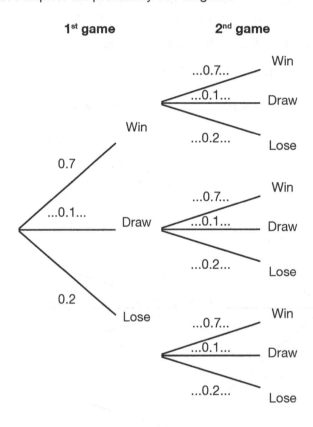

b) To find the probability that Tim will draw on both games, I simply follow the probability tree along the both draw branches (in bold below) and multiply each number I come across:

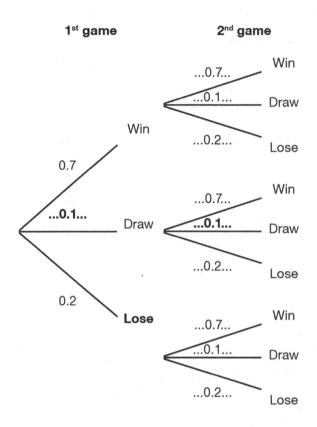

The probability of Tim having a draw on both games, using the AND rule, is:

P(1st *game draw* AND 2nd *game draw*) = 0.1 × 0.1 = 0.01

EXAMPLE

There are 20 sweets in a bag.

7 of the sweets are red

8 of the sweets are green

5 of the sweets are orange

If two sweets are taken out of the bag at random

a) Calculate the probability that the sweets will be the same colour.

b) Calculate the probability that the sweets will not be the same colour.

SOLUTION

a) The easiest way to answer this is to construct a probability tree diagram:

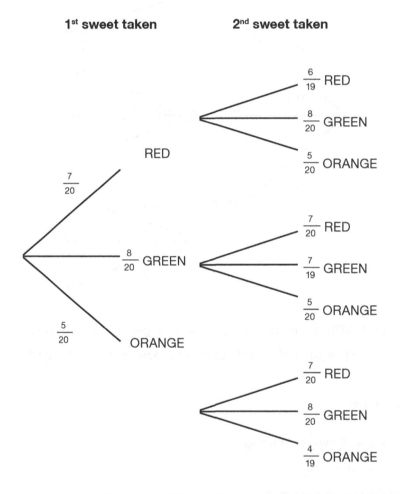

It is now easy to select the probabilities of two colours which are the same when taken out the bag:

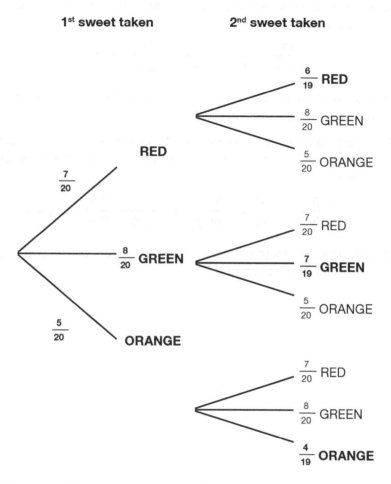

1ˢᵗ sweet taken   **2ⁿᵈ sweet taken**

To get the probability that the sweets will be the same colour, I need to multiply the probabilities for each colour from the first branch and the second, then add them all together:

$$\text{Red} = \frac{7}{20} \times \frac{6}{19} = \frac{21}{190}$$

$$\text{Green} = \frac{8}{20} \times \frac{7}{19} = \frac{14}{95}$$

$$\text{Orange} = \frac{5}{20} \times \frac{4}{19} = \frac{1}{19}$$

Adding all these probabilities to find the probability that sweets will be the same colour gives:

$$\frac{21}{190} + \frac{14}{95} + \frac{1}{19} = \frac{59}{190} = 0.31052$$

To two decimal places, the probability that the sweets will be the same colour when taken out the bag is 0.31

b) To find the probability that the sweets will **not** be the same colour I simply subtract 1 from the probability of the sweets being the same colour:

$$1 - \left(\frac{21}{190} + \frac{14}{95} + \frac{1}{19} \right) = 1 - \frac{59}{190} = \frac{131}{190} = 0.68947$$

To two decimal places, the probability that the sweets will not be the same colour when taken out the bag is 0.69

CHAPTER 32:
CIRCLES

This chapter will familiarise you with common formulas and theorems used when dealing with questions involving circles.

INTRODUCTION TO CIRCLES

The circumference of a circle is the entire outer edge distance around the whole circle.

The diameter of a circle is the distance from one end of a circle to another through the centre as shown below:

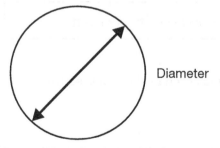

Diameter

The relationship between the circumference and diameter is that for any circle, the circumference is just over 3 times as large as the diameter. This is where the special number π 'pronounced as pie but spelt as pi' comes in. Its value is 3.1415926. It is common to use $\pi = 3.14$ in mathematical calculations.

The relationship between circumference and diameter (d) is therefore:

$$Circumference = \pi \times diameter = \pi \times d$$

A radius (r) of a circle is simply half the length of the diameter i.e. it extends from one edge of a circle to the centre of the circle only:

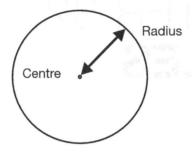

Because the radius is half the diameter, it would take 2 radiuses to make one diameter, so the formula can also be written in terms of radius:

$$Circumference = \pi \times 2 \ (radius) = 2\pi r$$

The radius (r) also appears in the formula for calculating the area of a circle:

$$Area \ of \ circle = \pi \times (r)^2 = \pi r^2$$

The area of a circle is 'pi' multiplied by the radius squared.

EXAMPLE
   a) The diameter of a circle is 5 cm, what is the circumference?

   b) The radius of a circle is 2.5 cm, what is the circumference?

   c) Use the radius in part b) to calculate the area of the circle.

Give your answers to 3 significant figures.

SOLUTION

a) The circumference can be calculated from the above formula:

$$Circumference = \pi \times diameter = \pi \times 5 \text{ cm}$$

I press the 'π' button on my calculator (note you may have to press shift first, depending on which calculator you are using) followed by the multiply sign, followed by 5 and I then press equals to get:

$$Circumference = \pi \times 5 \text{ cm} = 15.7 \text{ cm (3 significant figures)}$$

b) To calculate the circumference when given a radius (r), I need to use the formula:

$$Circumference = 2\pi r$$

I now substitute in the radius 2.5 cm and multiply with 2π to get:

$$Circumference = 2\pi(2.5) = \pi \times 5 = 15.7 \text{ cm (3 significant figures)}$$

This is the same answer as part a) which shows that the radius is half the diameter.

c) To calculate the area of the circle, given the radius of the circle, I need to use the formula:

$$Area \ of \ circle = \pi r^2$$

$$= \pi \times (2.5)^2$$

$$= 19.6 \text{ cm}^2$$

CIRCLE THEOREMS

There are two terms that are used frequently when discussing circle theorems, arc and subtended.

Subtended is the term used to describe two lines joining to form an angle, as shown below. The points from where the two lines originate can be used to describe what the angle is 'subtended' by or equally, the two lines may meet at the centre of the circle as shown below, in this case it is said that the angle is subtended at the centre of the circle.

An arc is a section of the circumference of a circle:

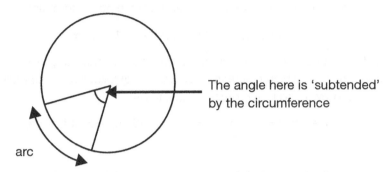

The angle here is 'subtended' by the circumference

arc

There are 7 circle theorems that you must familiarise yourself with for the exam:

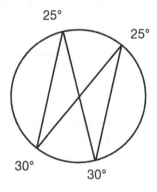

1. **The Bow Theorem** Angles which are subtended at the circumference and share the same arc are equal. Notice how the two top and two bottom angles separated by an arc are the same angles. This is the bow theorem.

2. **The Arrow Theorem** The angle subtended at the circumference of the circle is half that of the angle subtended at the centre of the circle. Notice how the angle at the centre is twice that of the angle at the circumference of the circle. This is known as the arrow theorem.

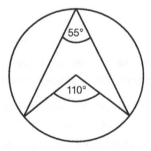

3. The Quad Theorem Opposite angles add up to 180°(see the two diagrams below)

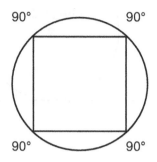 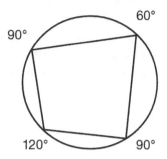

On the first diagram, both opposite angles are 90° and 90° + 90° = 180°

On the second diagram, 120° + 60° = 180° and 90° + 90° = 180°

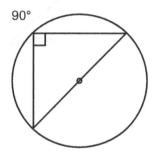

4. The angle in a semi- circle theorem The angle directly opposite the diameter line will always be 90°

5. The Alternate Segment Theorem The angle made by a tangent line (a line that just touches the outside of the circle) outside of the triangle is equal to the angle on the opposite side inside the triangle.

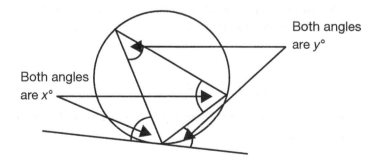

Both angles are $y°$

Both angles are $x°$

6. The Tangent Theorem 1

As mentioned above, a tangent is a straight line which touches the outside of the circle at one point. A tangent to a circle forms a right angle to the radius of the circle.

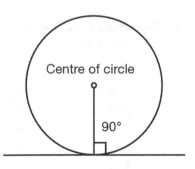

Centre of circle

90°

7. The Tangent Theorem 2

If two tangents are drawn on a circle and they intersect (as shown below), then the length of these two tangents are equal from the point of contact with the circle to the point where they meet.

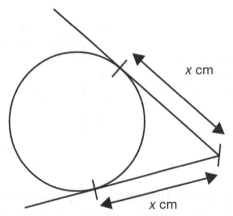

x cm

x cm

In the exam, questions may combine the use of all these rules or just use one or two. For practice, try the end of chapter questions, which combine the use of these theorems into one question.

ARCS AND SECTORS OF CIRCLES

A sector looks like a slice of cake. There are two types of sector, a minor sector and a major sector.

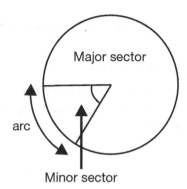

Given the radius of a circle and an angle of a sector, it is possible to calculate the length of the arc and the area of the sector

EXAMPLE

For the circle below, the radius is 5 cm and the sector has an angle of 40°. Calculate:

a) The area of the sector

b) The length of the minor arc

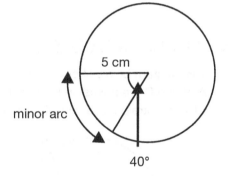

SOLUTION

a) A circle consists of 360°. The sector is 40° out of the total of 360° that the circle contains. I can write this as a fraction $\frac{40}{360}$

To calculate the area of the sector, I first calculate the area of the entire circle and multiply this by the fraction that the sector consists of, which I found to be $\frac{40}{360}$:

$$Area\ of\ circle = \pi r^2$$

$$= \pi \times (5)^2$$

$$= 25\pi$$

$$Area\ of\ sector = \frac{40}{360} \times 25\pi$$

Using a calculator, the answer is 8.73 cm²

b) To find the length of the minor arc, I use the same principal, except this time I need to calculate the circumference of the whole circle and then multiply this by the fraction $\frac{40}{360}$:

$$Circumference = 2\pi r$$

$$= 2\pi \times 5$$

$$= 10\pi$$

$$Length\ of\ arc = \frac{40}{360} \times 10\pi$$

Using a calculator, the answer is 3.49 cm

END OF CHAPTER QUESTIONS (CIRCLES)

1. The diagram below shows a circle with centre C.
   A, B and D are points on the circumference
   CBE is a straight line and DE is a tangent to the circle.

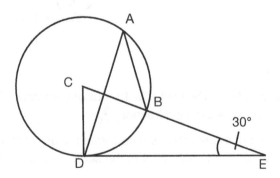

   a) Work out the size of angle DCE
   b) Work out the size of angle DAB
   c) Give reasons for your answers

*Remember with three letter angles, it is the letter in the middle which the question is asking you to find.

2.

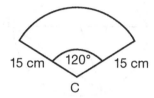

15 cm   120°   15 cm

C

The above diagram shows a sector of a circle, with its centre at C.

The radius of the circle is 15 cm and the angle of the sector is 120°

Calculate

    a) The area of the sector
    b) The length of the arc

Give your answers to 3 significant figures.

3.

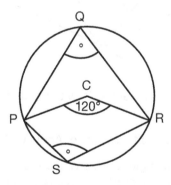

The above diagram is a circle; centre C, with points P, Q, R and S on the circumference.

Angle PQR = $x°$, Angle PCR=120° and Angle PSR=$y°$

    a) Write down the size of angle x, giving a reason for your answer
    b) Work out the size of angle y, giving a reason for your answer

4.

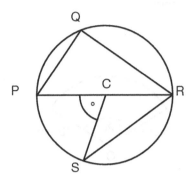

a) What is the size of angle PQR? Give a reason for your answer.
b) What is the size of angle PRS? Give a reason for your answer.

5.

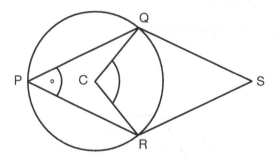

The circle shown above has a centre, C, with points P, Q and R lying on the circumference.

SQ and SR are both tangents to the circle. Angle QPR = 60°

a) Write down the angle QCR, giving a reason for your answer.
b) Calculate the angle QSR, giving a reason for your answer.

CHAPTER 33:
DIRECT AND INDIRECT PRO-PORTIONALITY

There are two types of relationship when it comes to proportionality, these are:

1. A direct relationship

2. An indirect relationship

The symbol used to represent 'is proportional to' in maths is $\propto$

A direct relationship has the form $a \propto b$

An indirect relationship has the form $a \propto \dfrac{1}{b}$

Where a and b represent quantities.

Questions involving direct and indirect relationships usually give the values of a and b and then ask you to find a formula for the relationship. This can easily be achieved as explained below.

For a direct relationship, replace the proportional sign, $\propto$, with an equals sign followed by a constant, k. This leads to:

$$a = kb$$

The quantities *a and b* can then be substituted into the above to find the value of *k*

For an indirect relationship, replace the proportional sign, ∝, with an equals sign followed by a constant, *k*. This leads to:

$$a = \frac{k}{b}$$

Once again, the quantities *a and b* can then be substituted into the above to find the value of *k*.

EXAMPLE

a is directly proportional to *b*

When *a* = 20, *b* = 10

   a) Find a formula for *b* in terms of *a*

   b) Calculate the value of *b* when *a* = 50

SOLUTION

   a) The question has stated that I am dealing with a 'directly proportional' relationship, which is in the form *a* ∝ *b*

As a formula, this becomes

$$a = kb$$

I know that *a* = 20 *and b* = 10. Substituting these values into the above formula leads to:

$$20 = k \times 10$$

$$k = \frac{20}{10} = 2$$

Now that I know *k* = 2, I can put this back into the formula *a* = *kb*, leading to a formula for *b* in terms of *a*:

$$a = 2b$$

   b) When *a* = 50:

$$50 = 2b$$

$$b = \frac{50}{2} = 25$$

EXAMPLE

a is indirectly proportional to *b*

When *a* = 20, *b* = 10

   c) Find a formula for *b* in terms of *a*

   d) Calculate the value of *b* when *a* = 50

SOLUTION

   c) The question has stated that I am dealing with an 'indirectly proportional' relationship, which is in the form $a \propto \frac{1}{b}$

As a formula, this becomes

$$a = \frac{k}{b}$$

I know that *a* = 20 *and b* = 10. Substituting these values into the above formula leads to:

$$20 = \frac{k}{10}$$

$$k = 20 \times 10 = 200$$

Now that I know *k* = 200 I can put this back into the formula *a* = *kb*, leading to a formula for *b* in terms of *a*:

$$a = \frac{200}{b}$$

  d) When *a* = 50:

$$50 = \frac{200}{b}$$

$$b = \frac{200}{50} = 4$$

END OF CHAPTER QUESTIONS
(DIRECT AND INDIRECT PROPORTIONALITY)

1. The money Sean earns in a week, y is directly proportional to the amount of hours he works, x.

If Sean earns £200 in a week and works 40 hours:

a) Find a formula for the amount of money Sean earns in a week

b) Calculate how much he earns if he works 20 hours in a week.

2. The amount Bob spends in a week, y is indirectly proportional to the amount he earns in a week, x.

If Bob spends £20 and earns £40 in a week:

a) Find a formula for the amount Bob spends in a week

b) Calculate how much he spends if he earns £50 in a week.

3. P is directly proportional to q

When $p = 200$, $q = 50$

a) Find a formula for p in terms of q

b) Calculate the value of q when $p = 400$

4. m is indirectly proportional to n

When $m = 20$, $n = 50$

a) Find a formula for m in terms of n

b) Calculate the value of n when $m = 400$

CHAPTER 34:
VECTORS

Vectors are used to represent direction between two points. Matrices are used to describe vectors and the examples in this chapter will introduce you to vector problems.

It is accepted, that when using vectors, the following directions are positive and negative:

Negative   Positive

Remember this, as it will become useful as you progress through this chapter.

An explanation of vectors is illustrated below:

Let's say I decide to move from point A to point B. The vector from point A to B is represented by <u>a</u>:

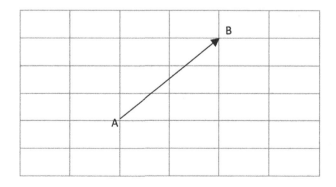

Vectors are usually described using matrices e.g. $\begin{pmatrix} x \\ y \end{pmatrix}$ where x represents horizontal movement and y represents vertical movement. So, for the vector $\underline{a}$:

$$\underline{a} = \begin{pmatrix} 2 \\ 3 \end{pmatrix}$$

This represents the fact that the line from point A to point B rises vertically by 3 units and horizontally by 2 units.

A negative sign in front of the matrix means that the line is now facing the opposite direction i.e. from B to A and not from A to B as it previously did.

EXAMPLE
On the grids, draw the vectors

$$\underline{a} = \begin{pmatrix} 2 \\ 3 \end{pmatrix} \text{ and } \underline{a} = -\begin{pmatrix} 2 \\ 3 \end{pmatrix}$$

SOLUTION

$$\underline{a} = \begin{pmatrix} 2 \\ 3 \end{pmatrix} \qquad\qquad \underline{a} = -\begin{pmatrix} 2 \\ 3 \end{pmatrix}$$

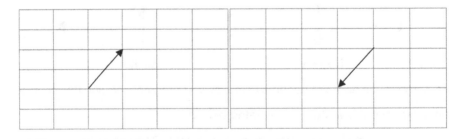

Note how the directions of the arrows have changed on both grids.

RESULTANT VECTORS

Let's say I want to go from point A to point C. I could either go through point B to get to point C or go straight from point A to point C, as shown:

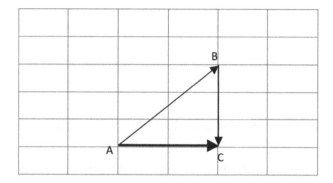

The line AB has vector $\underline{a}$ and the line BC has vector $\underline{b}$, because the line BC is facing in a negative direction, it has a negative sign in its vector, shown below:

$$\underline{a} = \begin{pmatrix} 2 \\ 3 \end{pmatrix}$$

$$\underline{b} = \begin{pmatrix} 0 \\ -3 \end{pmatrix}$$

The bold line is known as the resultant vector, $\underline{r}$

To find the vector $\underline{r}$ for the line AC, I need to add the two vectors $\underline{a} + \underline{b}$, this can be achieved by adding the top row numbers first and then the bottom row numbers.

$$\underline{r} = \underline{a} + \underline{b} = \begin{pmatrix} 2 \\ 3 \end{pmatrix} + \begin{pmatrix} 0 \\ -3 \end{pmatrix} = \begin{pmatrix} 2 \\ 0 \end{pmatrix}$$

Now, I will change the direction of the line BC on the grid and show you how to find the resultant.

As before, let's say I want to go from point A to point C. I could either go through point B to get to point C or go straight from point A to point C, as shown:

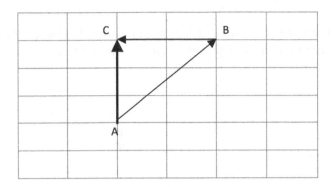

The bold line is called the resultant. To find the vector of the resultant line, I will need to add vectors $\underline{a}$ and $-\underline{b}$

Notice now how the vector $\underline{b}$ has a negative in front of it. This is because the line BC is pointing in a negative direction.

$$\underline{a} = \begin{pmatrix} 2 \\ 3 \end{pmatrix}$$

$$-\underline{b} = \begin{pmatrix} 2 \\ 0 \end{pmatrix}$$

$$\underline{r} = \underline{a} + (-\underline{b}) = \begin{pmatrix} 2 \\ 3 \end{pmatrix} + \begin{pmatrix} -2 \\ -0 \end{pmatrix} = \begin{pmatrix} 0 \\ 3 \end{pmatrix}$$

The resultant vector is positive as it is facing upwards i.e. in a positive direction, as explained at the beginning of the chapter.

Now that vectors have been introduced, examples of exam type questions are given below.

Note, vectors in this book are displayed with a line underneath the letter e.g. $\underline{b}$, however, in exams, the vector may simply be in bold print e.g. **b**

EXAMPLE

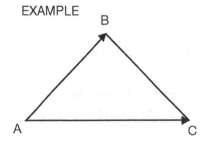

ABC is a triangle.

$\overrightarrow{AB} = \underline{a}$

$\overrightarrow{AC} = \underline{b}$

Find the vector $\overrightarrow{BC}$ in terms of $\underline{a}$ and $\underline{b}$

SOLUTION

To find the vector $\overrightarrow{BC}$, always start at the first letter, which in this case is B. I need to get to C, but must go through point A, as I do not know the vector BC.

To get from point B to point A, I must head downwards in a negative direction. The vector $\underline{a}$ is only positive when going from point A to point B, therefore the movement from point B to point A can be defined as a negative ($-\underline{a}$)

Now I am at point A and need to get to point C, this is a movement in the positive direction and can therefore be defined by the vector $\underline{b}$.

Therefore, the vector $\overrightarrow{BC} = -\underline{a} + \underline{b}$

EXAMPLE

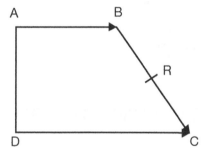

ABCD is a trapezium

$\overrightarrow{AB} = \underline{b}$

$\overrightarrow{BC} = \underline{c}$

$\overrightarrow{DC} = 2\overrightarrow{AB}$

Find, in terms of $\underline{b}$ and $\underline{c}$:

a) $\overrightarrow{AC}$

b) $\overrightarrow{CD}$

c) $\overrightarrow{AD}$

R is the point on BC such that BR : BC = 3 :1, find the following in terms of $\underline{b}$ and $\underline{c}$:

d) $\overrightarrow{AR}$

e) $\overrightarrow{RC}$

SOLUTION

a) $\overrightarrow{AC}$ means getting from A to B. To get from A to C, I need to get to the point B from A and then from B to C. To get to point B from A, I need to use the vector $\underline{b}$ and to get from point B to point C I need to use the vector $\underline{c}$.

Therefore, the entire movement from point A to point C is:

$$\overrightarrow{AC} = \underline{b} + \underline{c}$$

b) To get from point C to point D, I need to head in a negative direction. Also remember that CD is twice the length of AB. Therefore,

$$\overrightarrow{CD} = -2\underline{b}$$

c) To get from point A to D, the movement is:

$$\overrightarrow{AC} + \overrightarrow{CD}$$

These vectors were put in terms of $\underline{b}$ and $\underline{c}$ in parts a) and b) above. This makes it simple to find $\overrightarrow{AD}$.

$$\overrightarrow{AD} = \overrightarrow{AC} + \overrightarrow{CD} = \underline{b} + \underline{c} - 2\underline{b} = -\underline{b} + \underline{c}$$

d) $\overrightarrow{AR} = \underline{b} + \dfrac{3}{4}\underline{c}$

e) $\overrightarrow{RC} = \dfrac{1}{4}\underline{c}$

END OF CHAPTER QUESTIONS (VECTORS)

1.

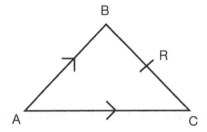

ABC is a triangle

$\overrightarrow{AB} = \underline{b}$

$\overrightarrow{AC} = \underline{c}$

a) Find the vector $\overrightarrow{BC}$ in terms of $\underline{b}$ and $\underline{c}$

R is a point on BC such that BR : BC = 5 : 3

b) Show that $\overrightarrow{AR} = \dfrac{1}{8}(3\underline{b} + 5\underline{c})$

2.

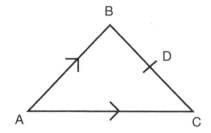

ABC is a triangle

D is the midpoint of BC and:

$\overrightarrow{AB} = \underline{b}$

$\overrightarrow{AC} = \underline{c}$

Find vector $\overrightarrow{AD}$ in terms of $\underline{b}$ and $\underline{c}$

3.

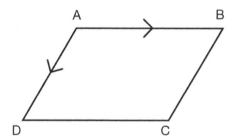

ABCD is a rhombus.

$\overrightarrow{AB} = \underline{b}$

$\overrightarrow{AD} = \underline{d}$

AB is parallel to DC and AD is parallel to BC.

Express, in terms of $\underline{b}$ *and* $\underline{d}$:

a) $\overrightarrow{BC}$

b) $\overrightarrow{BD}$

ANSWERS

TIMES TABLES ANSWERS

1. 4

2. 9

3. 4

4. 1

5. 0

6. 2

7. 9

8. 7

9. 6

10. 9

11. 2

12. 7

13. 0

14. 2

15. 2

16. 5

17. 4

18. 7

19. 8

20. 3

21. 1

22. 3

23. 4

24. 5

25. 5

26. 4

27. 6

END OF CHAPTER ANSWERS (LONG MULTIPLICATION)

1. 121

2. 156

3. 875

4. 26

5. 135

6. 90

7. 96

8. 675

9. 725

10. 2848

11. 284.8

12. 28.48

13. 2.848

14. 0.2848

15. 32472

16. 10710

17. 3.8064

18. 740

19. 46

20. 0.46

21. 0.046

END OF CHAPTER ANSWERS (LONG DIVISION)

1. 30

2. 32.5

3. 17.5

4. 7.5

5. 187.5

6. 447.5

7. 113.75

8. 222

9. 11.2

10. 14.75

11. 18

12. 7.5

13. 2.5

14. 111

15. 232.2

16. 177

17. 360

18. 35

19. 12

20. 85

21. 87.5

22. 8.75

END OF CHAPTER ANSWERS (DIRECTED NUMBERS)

1. 1

2. 2

3. 1

4. 0

5. 2

6. −8

7. −3

8. −12

9. 6

10. −3

11. 28

12. 98

13. −2

14. 7

15. 0

16. 20

17. 21

18. 24

19. 5

20. 15

21. 20

22. 20

23. 43

24. 7

25. 10

26. 0

27. 30

28. 21

29. 9

30. 15

31. 18

32. 4

33. 10

34. −8

35. −10

36. −20

37. 0

38. −63

39. −10

40. 10

41. 10

42. 8

43. 3

44. −2

45. −14

46. −12

47. −6

48. 6

49. −6

50. 3

51. −6

52. −2

53. −4

54. −4

55. 6

56. 5

57. −3

58. −4

59. −12

60. −13

61. −11

62. 144

63. −144

64. 144

65. 121

66. −32

67. 100

68. 150

69. −28

70. −4

END OF CHAPTER ANSWERS
(LOWEST COMMON MULTIPLE)

a) 30

b) 168

c) 90

d) 80

e) 16

f) 21

g) 30

h) 45

i) 30

j) 90

k) 126

l) 40

m) 40

n) 36

o) 30

p) 30

q) 56

r) 30

s) 400

END OF CHAPTER ANSWERS (FRACTIONS)

1. Let $x = 0.\dot{2}\dot{7}$ (same as 0.27272727...)

$100x = 27.27272727\ldots$

$100x - x = 99x = 27$

$$x = \frac{33}{99} = \frac{3}{11}$$

2. Let $x = 0.\dot{4}\dot{4}$ (same as 0.444444...)

$100x = 44.444444\ldots$

$100x - x = 99x = 44$

$$x = \frac{44}{99} = \frac{4}{9}$$

3. 0.5

4. 0.375

5. 0.75

7. $\dfrac{3}{8} + \dfrac{2}{5} = \dfrac{15}{40} + \dfrac{16}{40} = \dfrac{31}{40}$

8. 38

9. $\dfrac{3}{5} - \dfrac{1}{2} = \dfrac{6}{10} - \dfrac{5}{10} = \dfrac{1}{10}$

10. $2\dfrac{3}{5} - 1\dfrac{1}{2} = 2\dfrac{6}{10} - 1\dfrac{5}{10} = 1\dfrac{1}{10}$

11. $0.44 = \dfrac{44}{100} = \dfrac{11}{25}$

12. $\dfrac{5}{6} + \dfrac{1}{2} = \dfrac{5}{6} + \dfrac{3}{6} = \dfrac{8}{6} = 1\dfrac{2}{6} = 1\dfrac{1}{3}$

13. $\dfrac{5}{6} \div \dfrac{5}{6} = \dfrac{5}{6} \times \dfrac{6}{5} = 1$

14. $\dfrac{3}{8} \div \dfrac{9}{2} = \dfrac{3}{8} \quad \dfrac{2}{9} = \dfrac{1}{12}$

15. $2.5 = 2\dfrac{5}{10} = 2\dfrac{1}{2}$

Whereas

$2.2 = 2\dfrac{2}{10} = 2\dfrac{1}{5}$

(Remember that a decimal point followed by one digit means that digit is divided by 10 to become a fraction. This is why the statement is wrong.)

16. $3\dfrac{3}{8} \times 2\dfrac{2}{3} = \dfrac{27}{8} \times \dfrac{8}{3} = 9$ (both 8's cancel each other which leaves $\dfrac{27}{3} = 9$)

17. $\dfrac{1}{6} \times 48 = £8$ taken off the normal price of a ticket.

18. $2\dfrac{1}{8} + 1\dfrac{1}{2} = 2\dfrac{1}{8} + 1\dfrac{4}{8} = 3\dfrac{5}{8}$

19. To find which fractions are the smallest and which are the largest, find a common denominator for all fractions:

$\dfrac{1}{2}, \dfrac{2}{3}, \dfrac{1}{6}, \dfrac{3}{4} = \dfrac{6}{12}, \dfrac{8}{12}, \dfrac{2}{12}, \dfrac{9}{12}$

The fraction in order of size, from smallest to largest are:

$\dfrac{2}{12}, \dfrac{6}{12}, \dfrac{8}{12}, \dfrac{9}{12} = \dfrac{1}{6}, \dfrac{1}{2}, \dfrac{2}{3}, \dfrac{3}{4}$

20. $3\dfrac{1}{2} \times 2\dfrac{2}{3} = \dfrac{7}{2} \times \dfrac{8}{3} = \dfrac{28}{3} = 9\dfrac{1}{3}$

END OF CHAPTER ANSWERS (CALCULATING THE MODE, MEDIAN, MEAN, MOVING AVERAGES AND RANGE)

1. i) *Mean* $= \frac{320}{37.5} = 8.533$ minutes

ii) The median interval is $0 < t \leq 10$

iii) The modal interval is $0 < t \leq 10$

2. Median $= 7$

3. Median delay $= 0.5$ hours

4. Median interval height $= 2 < Y \leq 3$

5. Second 3-point moving average $= 35$

Third 3-point moving average $= 40$

The number of late students is on the increase.

6. Mean delay $= 1.56$ hours

7. Mean age $= 14$

END OF CHAPTER ANSWERS (CUMULATIVE FREQUENCY GRAPHS)

1. a) Plot points at (0,0), (20, 4), (40, 10), (60, 14), (80, 22), (100, 66), (120,102), (140,114) and (160,120)

Graph looks like:

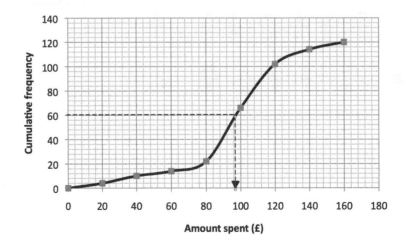

b) Median= £98 or thereabouts (dashed line above)

c) Visitors spent more throughout the year in cinema B because the median amount spent is higher.

2. a) To find cumulative frequency, start with 9 + 20 = 29 then 29+ 33 = 62 etc.

Time (t seconds)	Cumulative frequency
$0 < t \le 5$	9
$5 < t \le 10$	29
$10 < t \le 15$	62
$15 < t \le 20$	87
$20 < t \le 25$	100

b) Plot the points (0,0), (5, 9), (10, 29), (15, 62), (20, 87) and (25,100)

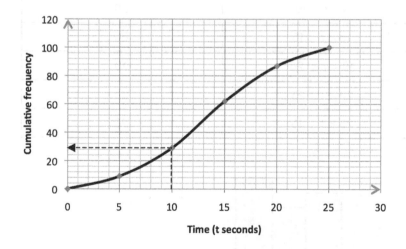

c) Approximately 28 students finished the maths challenge in 10 seconds or less (dashed line above) which means the rest of the students (100–28=72) students took more than 10 seconds to finish the maths challenge. You may find you do not get exactly 72 from the graph you have drawn, but any answer around 72 would be acceptable.

END OF CHAPTER ANSWERS (BOX PLOTS)

1. a) The greatest waiting time is 18 minutes

b) The median waiting time is 9 minutes

c) Interquartile range = 12 – 7 = 5

2. a) The median is 11

b) The upper quartile is 16.5

The lower quartile is 7

c) Smallest number is 3, largest number is 20

d) Box plot with lines at 7, 11 and 16.5 with whiskers extending from the box to the number 3 and   to the number 20.

END OF CHAPTER ANSWERS (HISTOGRAMS)

1. a)

Time (t hours)	Frequency
$0 < t \le 5$	55
$5 < t \le 10$	50
$10 < t \le 15$	60
$15 < t \le 20$	10
$20 < t \le 25$	25
$25 < t \le 45$	20

b)

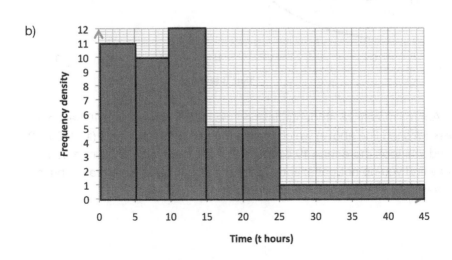

END OF CHAPTER ANSWERS (FREQUENCY POLYGONS)

1. Plot (2.5, 7), (7.5, 11), (15, 25), (30, 13) and (42.5, 9)

END OF CHAPTER ANSWERS (STEM AND LEAF DIAGRAMS)

1. a)

Stem	Leaf
1	5 6 7 8 9
2	0 1 2 3 5 7 8 9
3	1 3 4 6 9
4	2 3 5 7
5	2 2 5

Key
2 | 0 = 20

b) Median = 29

c) Lower quartile = $\dfrac{20 + 21}{2}$ = 20.5

Upper quartile = $\dfrac{42 + 43}{2}$ = 42.5

d) Mode is 52 seconds

END OF CHAPTER ANSWERS (RATIOS)

1. There are 35 raisin cookies in the jar.

2. 2:1

3. $\dfrac{60}{3}$ =20 m

4. a) The length of the shortest piece is 3 cm
   b) The length of the longest piece is 18 cm

5. Write the ratio as a fraction, and then simplify and rewrite the answer as a ratio:

$$\frac{26}{4} = 6\frac{2}{4} = 6\frac{1}{2} = \frac{13}{2}$$

which means the ratio is 13:2 in its simplest form.

6.

$$\frac{26}{6} = 4\frac{2}{6} = 4\frac{1}{3} = \frac{13}{3}$$

The ratio 26:6 in its simplest form is 13:3

7.

$$\frac{36}{14} = 2\frac{8}{14} = 2\frac{4}{7} = \frac{18}{3}$$

The ratio 36:14 in its simplest form is 18:7

END OF CHAPTER ANSWERS (STANDARD FORM)

1. 2.4×10^5

2. 1.6×10^5

3. 2.4×10^4

4. 1.6×10^4

5. 1400

6. 40 000

7. 2×10^{-5}

8. $2.4 \times 10^5 - 0.12 \times 10^5 = 2.28 \times 10^5$

9. $130 \times 10^4 - 130 \times 10^4 = 0$

10. 6×10^{-5}

END OF CHAPTER ANSWERS (QUADRATIC EQUATIONS)

1. $x = 1.33$ *or* $x = -3$

2. $x = 2.47$ *or* $x = -6.47$

3. $x = 6$ *or* $x = -1$

4. $x = 4$ *or* $x = -12$

5. $x = 2$ *or* $x = 4$

6. $x = -0.84$ *or* $x = -7.16$

7. $x = -4$ *or* $x = 2$

8. a) $x^2 - 5x + 6 = 12$, therefore $x^2 - 5x - 6 = 0$
     b) $x = 6$ *or* $x = -1$

9. a) $(x - 2)(x - 3)$
     b) $x = 2$ *or* $x = 3$

10. a)

$$\frac{2}{x - 2} - \frac{1}{x - 3} = \frac{1}{3}$$

$$2(x - 1) - (x - 2) = \frac{(x - 2)(x - 3)}{3}$$

$$2x - 2 - x + 2 = \frac{x^2 - 5x + 6}{3}$$

$$3(2x - 2 - x + 2) = x^2 - 5x + 6$$

$$6x - 6 - 3x + 6 = x^2 - 5x + 6$$

$$3x = x^2 - 5x + 6$$

$$x^2 - 5x + 6 - 3x = 0$$

$$x^2 - 8x + 6 = 0$$

   b) $x = 7.16$ *or* $x = 0.84$

END OF CHAPTER ANSWERS (FORMULAE AND HOW TO REARRANGE THEM)

1. $12y - 8$

2. $5y - 5z$

3. $27y + 18$

4. $2x^2 + 2xy$

5. $2(y - 2) + 5(y + 1) = (2y - 4) + (5y + 5) = 7y + 1$

6. $x + 7y$

7. $x = \dfrac{5y - 1}{2}$

8. $y = \dfrac{9}{2}F - z$

9. $T = 3x + 2y$

10. $z = 10$

END OF CHAPTER ANSWERS (INEQUALITIES)

1. $x > 3$

2. $x > 4$

3. $x < -9$

4. $x < -3$

5. $x < -\dfrac{2}{3}$

6. $x \le 3$

7. $x \ge 1$

8. $x \le 3$

9. $x \ge -3$

10. $x \le -14$

END OF CHAPTER ANSWERS (SURDS)

1. 8

2. 9

3. 9

4. 8

5. 3

6. 3

7. $12\sqrt{3}$

8. $12\sqrt{2}$

9. $2\sqrt{30}$

10. $2\sqrt{15}$

11. $(3 + \sqrt{5})(3 - \sqrt{5}) = 9 - 5 = 4$

12. $(4 + \sqrt{5})(4 - \sqrt{5}) = 4 - 5 = -1$

13. $(5 + \sqrt{5})(5 - \sqrt{5}) = 25 - 5 = 20$

14. $(2 + \sqrt{3})(2 - \sqrt{3}) = 4 - 3 = 1$

15. $(1 + \sqrt{5})(2 - \sqrt{5}) = 2 - \sqrt{5} + 2\sqrt{5} - 5 = -3 + \sqrt{5}$

16. $(9 + \sqrt{2})(2 - \sqrt{2}) = 18 - 9\sqrt{2} + 2\sqrt{2} - 2 = 16 - 7\sqrt{2}$

17. $(10 + \sqrt{8})(2 - \sqrt{2}) = (10 + 2\sqrt{2})(2 - \sqrt{2}) = 20 - 10\sqrt{2} + 4\sqrt{2} - 4 = 16 - 6\sqrt{2}$

18. $(9 + 4\sqrt{2})(2 - \sqrt{2}) = 18 - 9\sqrt{2} + 8\sqrt{2} - 8 = 10 - \sqrt{2}$

19. $(2 + 3\sqrt{3})(2 - 2\sqrt{3}) = 4 - 4\sqrt{3} + 6\sqrt{3} - 18 = -14 + 2\sqrt{3}$

20. $(5 + 5\sqrt{7})(2 - 4\sqrt{7}) = 10 - 20\sqrt{7} + 10\sqrt{7} - 140 = -130 - 10\sqrt{7}$

21. $\dfrac{1}{7 + \sqrt{5}} = \dfrac{7 - \sqrt{5}}{(7 + \sqrt{5})(7 - \sqrt{5})} = \dfrac{7 - \sqrt{5}}{49 - 25} = \dfrac{7 - \sqrt{5}}{24}$

(This cannot be reduced further so the answer remains in this form)

22. $\dfrac{1}{3 + \sqrt{5}} = \dfrac{3 - \sqrt{5}}{(3 + \sqrt{5})(3 - \sqrt{5})} = \dfrac{3 - \sqrt{5}}{(9 - 5)} = \dfrac{3 - \sqrt{5}}{4}$

23. $\dfrac{1}{2 + \sqrt{6}} = \dfrac{2 - \sqrt{6}}{(2 + \sqrt{6})(2 - \sqrt{6})} = \dfrac{2 - \sqrt{6}}{(4 - 6)} = \dfrac{2 - \sqrt{6}}{-2} = \dfrac{2}{-2} - \dfrac{\sqrt{6}}{2} = -1 - \dfrac{\sqrt{6}}{2}$

24. $\dfrac{1}{6 + \sqrt{10}} = \dfrac{6 - \sqrt{10}}{(6 + \sqrt{10})(6 - \sqrt{10})} = \dfrac{6 - \sqrt{10}}{(36 - 10)} = \dfrac{6 - \sqrt{10}}{26} = \dfrac{6}{26} - \dfrac{\sqrt{10}}{26} = \dfrac{3}{13} - \dfrac{\sqrt{10}}{26}$

25. $\dfrac{1}{7 - \sqrt{5}} = \dfrac{7 + \sqrt{5}}{(7 - \sqrt{5})(7 + \sqrt{5})} = \dfrac{7 + \sqrt{5}}{(49 - 5)} = \dfrac{7 + \sqrt{5}}{44}$

26. $\dfrac{1}{2 - \sqrt{10}} = \dfrac{2 + \sqrt{10}}{(2 - \sqrt{10})(2 + \sqrt{10})} = \dfrac{2 + \sqrt{10}}{(4 - 10)} = \dfrac{2 + \sqrt{10}}{-6} = \dfrac{2}{-6} + \dfrac{\sqrt{10}}{-6} = -\dfrac{1}{3} - \dfrac{\sqrt{10}}{6}$

27. $\dfrac{1}{4 + 2\sqrt{7}} = \dfrac{4 - 2\sqrt{7}}{(4 + 2\sqrt{7})(4 - 2\sqrt{7})} = \dfrac{4 - 2\sqrt{7}}{(16 - 28)} = \dfrac{4 - 2\sqrt{7}}{-12} = \dfrac{4}{-12} - \dfrac{2\sqrt{7}}{-12} = -\dfrac{1}{3} + \dfrac{\sqrt{7}}{6}$

28. $\dfrac{1}{3 - 2\sqrt{3}} = \dfrac{3 + 2\sqrt{3}}{(3 - 2\sqrt{3})(3 + 2\sqrt{3})} = \dfrac{3 + 2\sqrt{3}}{(9 - 12)} = \dfrac{3 + 2\sqrt{3}}{-3} = \dfrac{3}{-3} + \dfrac{2\sqrt{3}}{-3} = -1 - \dfrac{2\sqrt{3}}{3}$

29. $\dfrac{2}{4+\sqrt{5}} = \dfrac{2(4-\sqrt{5})}{(4+\sqrt{5})(4-\sqrt{5})} = \dfrac{8-2\sqrt{5}}{(16-5)} = \dfrac{8-2\sqrt{5}}{11}$

30. $\dfrac{7}{11-2\sqrt{10}} = \dfrac{7(11+2\sqrt{10})}{(11-2\sqrt{10})(11+2\sqrt{10})} = \dfrac{77+14\sqrt{10}}{(121-40)} = \dfrac{77+14\sqrt{10}}{81}$

31. $\dfrac{3}{2+3\sqrt{3}} = \dfrac{3(2-3\sqrt{3})}{(2+3\sqrt{3})(2-3\sqrt{3})} = \dfrac{6-9\sqrt{3}}{(4-27)} = \dfrac{6-9\sqrt{3}}{-23} = -\dfrac{(6-9\sqrt{3})}{-23}$

32. $\dfrac{2+\sqrt{3}}{2-\sqrt{3}} = \dfrac{2+\sqrt{3}}{2-\sqrt{3}} \times \dfrac{2-\sqrt{3}}{2+\sqrt{3}} = \dfrac{4-3}{4-3} = 1$

33. $\dfrac{3+\sqrt{3}}{7+\sqrt{3}} = \dfrac{3+\sqrt{3}}{7+\sqrt{3}} \times \dfrac{7-\sqrt{3}}{7-\sqrt{3}} = \dfrac{21-3\sqrt{3}+7\sqrt{3}-3}{49-3} = \dfrac{18}{46} + \dfrac{4\sqrt{3}}{46} = \dfrac{9}{23} + \dfrac{2\sqrt{3}}{23}$

34. $\dfrac{5+3\sqrt{3}}{2-2\sqrt{3}} = \dfrac{5+3\sqrt{3}}{2-2\sqrt{3}} \times \dfrac{2+2\sqrt{3}}{2+2\sqrt{3}} = \dfrac{10+10\sqrt{3}+6\sqrt{3}+18}{4-12} = \dfrac{28}{-8} + \dfrac{16\sqrt{3}}{-8} = -\dfrac{7}{2} - 2\sqrt{3}$

35. $\dfrac{3-7\sqrt{3}}{8+\sqrt{3}} = \dfrac{3-7\sqrt{3}}{8+\sqrt{3}} \times \dfrac{8-\sqrt{3}}{8-\sqrt{3}} = \dfrac{24-3\sqrt{3}-56\sqrt{3}+21}{64-3} = \dfrac{45}{61} - \dfrac{59\sqrt{3}}{61} = \dfrac{45-59\sqrt{3}}{61}$

36. $\dfrac{10+3\sqrt{8}}{7-\sqrt{8}} = \dfrac{10+3\sqrt{8}}{7-\sqrt{8}} \times \dfrac{7+\sqrt{8}}{7-\sqrt{8}} = \dfrac{70+10\sqrt{8}+21\sqrt{8}+24}{49-8} = \dfrac{94}{41} - \dfrac{31\sqrt{8}}{41} = \dfrac{94-62\sqrt{2}}{41}$

37. $\dfrac{4-2\sqrt{3}}{5-6\sqrt{3}} = \dfrac{4-2\sqrt{3}}{5-6\sqrt{3}} \times \dfrac{5+6\sqrt{3}}{5+6\sqrt{3}} = \dfrac{20+24\sqrt{3}-10\sqrt{3}+36}{25-108} = \dfrac{56}{-83} + \dfrac{14\sqrt{3}}{-83} = -\dfrac{56}{83} - \dfrac{14\sqrt{3}}{83}$

END OF CHAPTER ANSWERS (INDICES)

1. 1

2. 1

3. 1

4. 1

5. 1

6. $\dfrac{1}{16}$

7. $\dfrac{1}{9}$

8. $\dfrac{1}{25}$

9. $\dfrac{1}{8}$

10. 16

11. 4

12. 1

13. $4^{-5} = \dfrac{1}{4^5} = \dfrac{1}{1024}$

14. 16

15. x^6

16. b^8

17. $y(xy^2 \times yx^4) = y(x^5y^3) = x^5y^4$

18. x^6

19. xy

20. $x^{15}y^3z^6$

21. $xz^2 + x^4yz$

22. $p^4ra + p^2qr^5a^3$

23. z

24. $x^{1/4}$

25. $x^{1/2}y$

END OF CHAPTER ANSWERS (FACTORISATION)

1. $(x + 3)(x + 4)$

2. $(x +1)(x -2)$

3. $(x +2)(x +3)$

4. $(x -3)(x -5)$

5. $(x -1)(x -3)$

6. $(3x + 2)(3x + 2) = (3x + 2)^2$

7. $(x + y)(x - y)$

8. $(x - 4)(x + 2)$

9. $3x(4 - x)$

10. $(x + 2)(x + 6)$

11. $(x + 5)(x - 5)$

12. $(2x + 3)(2x - 3)$

END OF CHAPTER ANSWERS (SEQUENCES/ NTH TERMS)

1. 0   7   26   63

2. a) 15
b) 7
c) The numbers in the sequence are all odd and because 2 is subtracted each time, the numbers in the sequence remain odd. 6 is an even number and therefore cannot be included in the sequence.

3. 6n

4. $3 + (n - 1)2 + (n - 1)(n - 2)$

END OF CHAPTER ANSWERS (SIMULTANEOUS EQUATIONS)

1. $x = 3, y = 4$

2. $x = 3, y = 2$

3. $x = 2, y = 0$

4. $x = 3, y = 7$

5. $x = 1, y = 2$

6. $x = -1, y = 2$

7. $x = -4, y = 5$

END OF CHAPTER ANSWERS (STRAIGHT LINE GRAPHS)

1. $y = \frac{1}{2}x + 5$

2. $y = \frac{5}{6}x + \frac{4}{3}$

3. $y = \frac{2}{3}x + 3$

4. a)

x	-2	-1	0	1	2
y	-3	-1	1	3	5

b) Graph looks like:

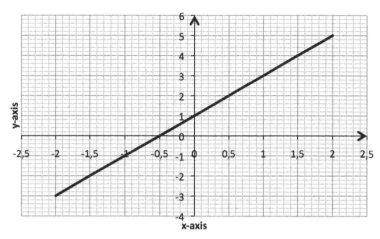

5. $y = \dfrac{2}{3}x + 2$

END OF CHAPTER ANSWERS (GRAPH TRANSFORMATIONS)

1. $y = f(x) - 5$

2. a) The graph of $y = sin(x)$ is stretched in the y-axis by a factor of 2 and stretched in the x-axis by a factor of $\dfrac{1}{2}$

b) Graph looks like (dashed curve):

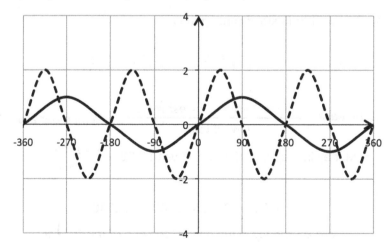

3. Equation of the curve becomes $f(x + 8)$

END OF CHAPTER ANSWERS:
(PYTHAGORAS THEOREM AND THE USE OF SIN, COS AND TAN IN RIGHT ANGLED TRIANGLES)

1. a) $AC^2 = AB^2 + BC^2 = 2^2 + 3^2 = 4 + 9 = 13$

$AC = \sqrt{13} = 3.61$ cm

b) $\text{Tan}A = \dfrac{BC}{AB} = \dfrac{3}{2} = 1.5$

$A = \tan^{-1}(1.5) = 56.3°$

2. a) $AC^2 = AB^2 + BC^2 = 10^2 + 5^2 = 100 + 25 = 125$

$AC = \sqrt{125} = 11.2$ cm

b) $\text{Tan}A = \dfrac{5}{10} = 0.5$

$A = \tan^{-1}(0.5) = 26.6°$

END OF CHAPTER ANSWERS
(USING SIN, COS AND TAN IN TRIANGLES THAT ARE NOT RIGHT ANGLED)

1. a) $AC = 20.7$ cm
b) Area $= 70.5$ cm^2

2. Angle XYZ $= 96.9°$ (3 significant figures)

3. Angle $x = 74.6°$ (3 significant figures)

END OF CHAPTER ANSWERS (PERCENTAGES)

1.

$\text{\% increase} = \dfrac{highest\ value - lowest\ value}{lowest\ value}$ *Remember* 2% = 0.02

a) Money in the bank after the 1st year: $0.02 = \dfrac{x - £2000}{£2000}$

$x = (0.02 \times £2000) + £2000 = £2040$

Where x = money in the bank at the end of the 1st year

b) Money in the bank after the 2nd year: $0.02 = \dfrac{y - £2040}{£2040}$

$y = (0.02 \times £2040) + £2040 = £2080.80$

Where y = money in the bank at the end of the 2nd year

2. *Total amount after n years = Original amount* $\times$ *(1+* $\dfrac{\%interest}{100}$ *)^n*

So, for this question, the formula becomes:

$$£3499.20 = £3000 \times (1 + \dfrac{8}{100})^n$$

$$£3499.20 = £3000 \times (1 + 0.08)^n$$

$$£3499.20 = £3000 \times (1.08)^n$$

$$\dfrac{£3499.20}{£3000} = (1.08)^n$$

$$£1.1664 = (1.08)^n$$

$$n = 2$$

3. £587.50

4.

$$\% \; decrease = \dfrac{highest \; value - lowest \; value}{highest \; value}$$

Price at the end of 1st year:

$$0.02 = \dfrac{£7000 - lowest \; value}{£7000}$$

Lowest value (end of year 1) = £6860

Price at the end of 2nd year:

$$0.02 = \dfrac{£6860 - lowest \; value}{£6860}$$

Lowest value (end of year 2) = £6722.80

Price at the end of 3rd year:

$$0.02 = \frac{£6722.80 - lowest\ value}{£6722.80}$$

Lowest value (end of year 3) = £6588.34

The car is worth £6588.34 at the end of the 3 years.

END OF CHAPTER ANSWERS (EXCHANGE RATES, VALUE FOR MONEY AND TIME TO EMPTY TANK PROBLEMS)

1. €325.50

2. £95.20

3. 120 seconds

4. 240 seconds

5. Purchasing a pack of 10 cans for £5 means that every can is worth 50p, whereas purchasing a pack of 5 cans for £3 means that every can is worth 60p. Therefore, purchasing the pack of 10 cans is better value for money as every can costs 50p rather than 60p.

END OF CHAPTER ANSWERS (UPPER AND LOWER BOUNDS)

1. Area of a square is found by multiplying two lengths of a square together.

   Lower bound of square length = 2.35 cm
   Upper bound of square length = 2.45 cm

   a) Lower bound area of square = 2.35 × 2.35 = 5.5225 cm^2
   b) Upper bound area of square = 2.45 × 2.45 = 6.0025 cm^2

2. Upper bound of 150 = 150.5
Lower bound of 150 = 145.5

3. Area of rectangle $= 10 \times x$

$$x = \frac{\textit{Area of rectangle}}{10}$$

a) To calculate the upper bound for the length x, find the upper bound of the area of the rectangle and the lower bound for the length 10 cm:

Upper bound for area of rectangle = 240.5 cm²
Lower bound for length 10 cm = 9.5 cm

$$\textit{Upper bound for length } x = \frac{240.5}{95} = 25.31578947$$

b) To calculate the lower bound for length x, find the lower bound of the area of the rectangle and the upper bound for the length 10 cm:

Lower bound for area of rectangle = 239.5 cm²
Upper bound for length 10 cm = 10.5 cm

$$\textit{Lower bound for length } x = \frac{239.5}{10.5} = 25.31578947$$

END OF CHAPTER ANSWERS (PROBABILITY)

1. a)

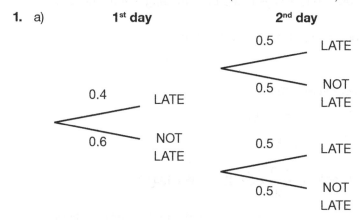

Remember the and/or rules for probability: AND means multiply, OR means add.

b) P (Late on 1st day **and** Late on 2nd day) = 0.4 × 0.5 = 0.20

c) P (Not late on 1st day **and** Not late on 2nd day) = 0.6 × 0.5 = 0.3

d) P (Late on just 1 day) =

P (late 1st day **and** not late 2nd day) **or** P (not late 1st day **and** late 2nd day)

= 0.4 × 0.5 + 0.6 × 0.5

= 0.2 + 0.3 = 0.5

END OF CHAPTER ANSWERS (CIRCLES)

1. a) Angle DCE = 180° − 90° − 30° = 60° (Using tangent theorem 1)

b) Angle DAB=30°

c) For angle DCE a tangent to a circle always makes a right angle, which makes the triangle EDC a right angled triangle and because all the angles in a triangle add up to 180° it is easy to find the remaining angle.

For angle DAB, the arc BD makes an angle at both the centre, C and the circumference A. When an arc is shared between an angle at the centre and an angle at the circumference, the angle at the circumference is always half that of the angle at the centre.

Therefore, angle DAB $=\dfrac{1}{2}$ × 60° = 30°

2. a) *Area of circle* = πr^2

$$= \pi \times (15)^2$$

$$=225\pi$$

$$Area\ of\ sector = \dfrac{120}{360} \times 225\pi = 235.619449$$

$$= 236\ cm^2\ (3\ significant\ figures)$$

b) *Circumference* $= 2\pi r$

$$= 2\pi \times 15$$

$$= 30\pi$$

Length of arc $= \dfrac{120}{360} \times 30\pi = 31.41592654$ cm

$=31.4$ cm (3 significant figures)

3. a) $x = 60°$

Using the arrow theorem, the angle x is half the size of the angle at the centre.

b) $y° = 60°$

PCRS is a cyclic quadrilateral. Using the quad theorem, opposite angles in a cyclic quadrilateral must add up to 180°, a cyclic quadrilateral being a quadrilateral where all four sides touch the circumference of the circle. Because the centre angle is 120°, the opposite angle, $y°$, must be 60° so they both add up to 180°.

4. a) Angle PQR $= 90°$

Using the angle in a semi circle theorem, the angle opposite a diameter line will always be 90°.

b) Angle PRS $= 30°$

Angles on a straight line add up to 180°. Which means that the angle inside the triangle RCS is 120°:

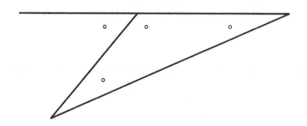

Secondly, both lines CS and RS are equal in length because they are both radiuses of the circle. Both lines leave from the centre of the circle to the circumference and therefore can only be the same length. This means that both the angles R and S are equal.

Because angles in a triangle add up to 180°, it is possible to subtract 180° from 120° to find the remaining angles.

180°–120°=60°, dividing this by 2 now gives a value for both angle R and S:

$$\frac{60}{2} = 30°$$

This means that angle PRS is 30°

5. a) Angle QCR = 120°. This is because of the arrow theorem, which states that the angle at the circumference is half that of the angle at the centre of the circle.

b) Angle QSR=60°

QSRC is a quadrilateral which can be split in half (red dashed line below), giving two triangles with a central angle of 60° each. The two tangents make angles of 90° where they meet the circle at Q and R, giving both triangles angles of 90° each:

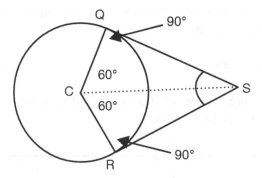

Angles in triangle must add up to 180°, so to find angle QSC:

Angle QSC = 180° – 90° – 60° = 30°

Angle CSR = 180° – 90° – 60° = 30°

This makes the total angle QSR: 30° + 30° = 60°

Alternatively, you could use the fact that all angles in a quadrilateral add up to 360° and so the calculation to find QSR would be:

$$360° - 90° - 90° - 120° = 60°$$

END OF CHAPTER ANSWERS (DIRECT AND INDIRECT PROPORTIONALITY)

1. a) $y = 5x$

b) £100

2. a) $y = \dfrac{800}{x}$

b) £16

3. a) $p = 4q$

b) 100

4. a) $m = \dfrac{1000}{n}$

b) 0.4

END OF CHAPTER ANSWERS (VECTORS)

1. a) $\overrightarrow{BC} = -\underline{b} + \underline{c}$

b) $\overrightarrow{AR} = \overrightarrow{AB} + \overrightarrow{BR}$

$$= \underline{b} + \frac{5}{8}(-\underline{b} + \underline{c})$$
$$= \underline{b} - \frac{5}{8}\underline{b} + \frac{5}{8}\underline{c}$$
$$= \frac{3}{8}\underline{b} + \frac{5}{8}\underline{c}$$
$$= \frac{1}{8}(3\underline{b} + 5\underline{c})$$

2. First find $\overrightarrow{BC}$

$$\overrightarrow{BC} = -\underline{b} + \underline{c}$$

$$\overrightarrow{AD} = \overrightarrow{AB} + \frac{1}{2}\overrightarrow{BC}$$

$$= \underline{b} + \frac{1}{2}(-\underline{b} + \underline{c})$$

$$= \frac{1}{2}\underline{b} + \frac{1}{2}\underline{c}$$

Because AD and BC are parallel, the vectors are the same,

a) $\overrightarrow{BC} = \underline{d}$

b) To get from point B to point D, first go from point B to C then from point C to point D.

Because AB and DC are parallel, the vector on DC is the same as that on AB.

$$\overrightarrow{BD} = \underline{d} - \underline{b}$$

DISCLAIMER

Every effort has been made to ensure that the information contained within this guide is accurate at the time of publication. How2become Ltd are not responsible for anyone failing any part of any exam or selection process as a result of the information contained within this guide. How2become Ltd and their authors cannot accept any responsibility for any errors or omissions within this guide, however caused. No responsibility for loss or damage occasioned by any person acting, or refraining from action, as a result of the material in this publication can be accepted by How2become Ltd.

how2become

Visit www.how2become.co.uk to find
more titles and courses that will help you to pass
any job interview or selection process:

- Online GCSE testing suite
- Job interview DVDs and books
- 1-day intensive career training courses
- Psychometric testing books and CDs.

www.how2become.co.uk

NOTES

NOTES